EUROPE'S
FINANCIAL CRISIS

EUROPE'S FINANCIAL CRISIS

A SHORT GUIDE TO HOW THE EURO FELL INTO CRISIS AND THE CONSEQUENCES FOR THE WORLD

JOHN AUTHERS

Vice President, Publisher: Tim Moore
Associate Publisher and Director of Marketing: Amy Neidlinger
Executive Editor: Jim Boyd
Editorial Assistant: Pamela Boland
Development Editor: Russ Hall
Operations Specialist: Jodi Kemper
Assistant Marketing Manager: Megan Graue
Cover Designer: Chuti Prasertsith
Cover Photograph: ©artSILENSE.com/Fotolia.com
Managing Editor: Kristy Hart
Senior Project Editor: Lori Lyons
Copy Editor: Apostrophe Editing Services
Proofreader: Kathy Ruiz
Indexer: Lisa Stumpf
Senior Compositor: Gloria Schurick
Manufacturing Buyer: Dan Uhrig

First Printing November 2012

ISBN-10: 0-13-313371-0
ISBN-13: 978-0-13-313371-4

Pearson Education LTD.
Pearson Education Australia PTY, Limited.
Pearson Education Singapore, Pte. Ltd.
Pearson Education Asia, Ltd.
Pearson Education Canada, Ltd.
Pearson Educación de Mexico, S.A. de C.V.
Pearson Education—Japan
Pearson Education Malaysia, Pte. Ltd.

Library of Congress Cataloging-in-Publication Data

Authers, John, 1966-
  Europe's financial crisis : short guide to how the euro fell into crisis, and the consequences for the world / John Authers. — 1st ed.
    p. cm.
  ISBN 978-0-13-313371-4 (pbk. : alk. paper)
  1. European Union countries—Economic conditions—21st century. 2. Monetary policy—European Union countries. 3. Banks and banking—European Union countries. 4. Global Financial Crisis, 2008-2009. I. Title.
  HC240.A98 2013
  330.94—dc23
                                                2012025668

Dedicted to the memory of
Manuel de LaVega

Contents

Acknowledgments

I want to thank the FT Press, led by my editor Jim Boyd, and including Russ Hall and Lori Lyons, for helping to shape this work, as have the editors with whom I have worked on updating *The Fearful Rise of Markets* for its translations into Korean and Mandarin. I am grateful to the many audiences, in the U.S. and the U.K., to whom I presented my ideas about the first book, which helped shape my opinions about how to navigate the far trickier landscape that has followed the implosion of 2008 and its immediate rebound. For shaping my ideas about the Eurozone, I particularly want to thank George Magnus, Michala Marcussen, Ashraf Laidi, Holger Schmieding, Simon Derrick, Jane Foley, and Mike Gallagher. In particular, I must thank the *Financial Times*, my employer now for 22 years. It has given me the perfect vantage point from which to view the tectonic shifts in world markets. I spent much of the last two years running the FT's great Lex Column, an honor for me, and I learned much from my colleagues there. I have also worked ever more with the growing video department and learned many valuable lessons about presenting often complicated ideas in new media. I also thank the staff at Fort Washington Library in Manhattan. Although I now live in London, I again found that it provided a great venue for writing this

book during a return trip to New York, just as it had done the first time around.

Most of all, I am grateful to my family. That gratitude is particularly great because of the turn life took for me after I completed the manuscript for *The Fearful Rise of Markets*. Shortly afterward, and only days before the book was published, I was hospitalized with an attack of acute pancreatitis that might easily have killed me. Subsequently, I endured many months of slow convalescence. I am thankful that both my employer and my family stood by me during this dreadful episode, and that my return to health is almost complete.

A brush with mortality can, however, have its advantages. It makes it easy to be detached about the often terrifying events in the world markets. And it helps reveal, like nothing else, what really matters in life. My heartfelt thanks to my children, Andie, Josie, and Jamie. Most of all, I wish to thank my wife, Sara Silver. Quite apart from everything else, she has also been my best and strictest editor, immeasurably improving this book. Thank you, Sara.

About the Author

John Authers, Senior Investment Columnist for the *Financial Times*, is responsible for the weekly "Long View" and other columns on markets and investment. One of the world's most influential financial journalists, he has served as global head of the *Financial Times* "Lex" column, U.S. markets editor, Mexico City bureau chief, and U.S. banking correspondent.

Authers speaks worldwide and appears frequently on major U.S. and global media, including the BBC, CNN, MSNBC, NPR, and PBS. He has twice been honored as the U.K.'s Investment Journalist of the Year and was named the Wincott Foundation's Senior Financial Journalist of the year for 2009, the premier award in British financial journalism. He is author of *The Fearful Rise of Markets: Global Bubbles, Synchronized Meltdowns, and How to Prevent Them in the Future*, to which this e-book is a sequel.

Authers's previous book, *The Victim's Fortune*, coauthored with Richard Wolffe, earned the prestigious Best of Knight-Bagehot Award.

Introduction

This brief e-book started as an update and sequel to *The Fearful Rise of Markets*, which was published in early 2010. That book described how a giant speculative bubble came to encompass virtually all world markets and then burst. It followed the story until the end of 2009, when markets were bouncing back.

Now, writing in the summer of 2012 more than three years after markets hit bottom, the crisis has migrated across the Atlantic. Its epicenter is in the Eurozone, which is the center of this book. It can be read in its own right, telling the story of how Europe slipped into crisis, how developments in the United States and the emerging markets contributed to its problems, and why this matters for the rest of the world, notably the United States. For a full discussion of how the world got into its mess in the first place, please turn to my earlier book.

1

What has happened in Europe? Put briefly, Europe created a single currency before its member nations were ready for it. Their economies had not converged sufficiently for one currency to fit all. As a result, the common currency tended perversely to push the nations further apart, with the nations of the periphery, such as Spain and Ireland, booming unsustainably. They developed huge trade deficits with Germany as they sucked in imports and then crashed. This created a necessary condition for the crisis.

The second was Europe's huge and bloated banking system. Unlike in the United States, European banks were allowed to grow huge, and to spread into diverse financial businesses, with the tacit backing of their governments. As a result, the banks became far too big for their host governments to rescue with any ease.

The catalyst for the Eurozone's troubles came with the U.S. credit crisis. Wall Street had long made unnaturally big profits by repackaging debt backed by subprime U.S. mortgages and selling it to European banks. When the crisis hit, it was obvious that Europe's banks were sitting on losses and might need help from their governments to repair their balance sheets. That in turn called into question whether nations could repay their sovereign debts. In such situations, a government usually just prints money and devalues its currency, making the debt easier to pay. But for all those countries using the euro, this was no longer possible.

When Greece revealed that it could no longer finance its deficit, European politicians' initial response was to bail it out, while forcing Greece to make painful austerity cuts, and coming up with a new fund of money that could finance future bail-outs. The idea was that this would convince the markets that the problem could be contained. It failed. Instead, other countries—Ireland, Portugal and Spain—also needed help, raising doubts whether the money existed to help them, while austerity in Greece proved counter-productive. It may have reduced government spending, but by cutting into economic activity it reduced tax revenues as well.

Now, the problem is essentially political. More austerity seems politically untenable—voters will no longer accept it. So if the Eurozone wants to avoid exits by any of its current members, there appear to be only two options. Either the European Central Bank can simply print the money to pay the debts (which in the long-term would be inflationary); or all the countries in the Eurozone can agree to stand behind all its countries' debts. This latter option, often referred to as "eurobonds," would solve the problem, because the Eurozone as a whole is solvent. But it would need a new European treasury department of some kind, which means loss of sovereignty for many countries, and it would also imply that taxpayers of Europe's stronger nations would have to bail out their weaker brethren.

Investors must now bet on whether politicians can possibly find a compromise.

The prospect of default by any European country terrifies markets. Why? Such defaults would probably trigger the collapse of Europe's banking system because banks are heavily leveraged and hold huge piles of government bonds, bought on the assumption that they are risk-free. That would damage other banking systems around the world. Any economy that suffered a default or took on a new currency would immediately lapse into a severe economic recession, with ripple effects for banks and exporters across the world. Just as the financial crisis that followed the Lehman Brothers bankruptcy created an immediate seizure in trade and economic activity worldwide, there is every reason to fear that a Euro-exit (a decision by one or more Eurozone member countries to abandon the euro and revert to their own currency) would have the same effect. The most alarming possibility is a disorderly break-up of the euro, an event for which there is no precedent. Markets would find it hard to cope, and economic activity would be likely to stall; one estimate by ING, a big European insurer, is that in these conditions, every country in the Eurozone would suffer a decline of more than 10 percent in their gross domestic product.[1] That implies a far deeper recession even than the depression of the 1930s, and would inevitably inflict a severe recession on the United States. This is why Europe's crisis now so dominates the world's attention.

Evidently, it is impossible to understand events in the Eurozone without understanding the credit crisis and how it started in the United States with the market for subprime mortgages. I therefore summarize here, in the second chapter, the conclusions of *The Fearful Rise* as to how that came about. For a full discussion, look at that earlier book.

What of the United States? On the surface, it has recovered well. Stocks are roughly double their lows of early 2009. But the dissonance with European markets is a huge clue that all is not well. Stock markets like Spain's have fallen below even their lowest levels from the post-Lehman crisis. The elevated level of U.S. stocks implies extreme confidence either that European investors have wildly exaggerated the risks or that Europe's problems need not harm the United States. Both propositions are dubious. In fact, U.S. markets may merely be responding to the copious flows of cheap money that the Federal Reserve has pumped into the system.

Beyond Europe, it is worrisome that markets for different kinds of assets still march in lockstep. Whole asset classes—foreign exchange, commodities, bonds, and equities—have shifted in line with each other, apparently all responding to cues from the Federal Reserve.

The initial rebound was so tightly synchronized that prices of the most important building blocks of the economy must have been set inefficiently.

This was a central theme of *The Fearful Rise*, and it matters because inefficiently priced markets drove the global market crash of 2008, which led to the global economic seizure in 2009. If currencies are buoyed or depressed by speculation, they skew the terms of global trade. A government's capability to run its own economy is compromised if exchange rates make goods too cheap or too expensive. An excessive oil price can drive the world into recession. Extreme food prices mean starvation for billions. Money pouring into emerging markets stokes inflation and destabilizes the economies on which the world now relies for growth. Credit that is too cheap leads to an unsustainable boom and then an inevitable bust, when credit is tightened and becomes too expensive for borrowers. And for investors who seek stability through diversification, risk management becomes impossible when all markets move in unison. With nowhere to hide, everyone's pension plan suffers if markets crash together. In one week in October 2008, the value of global retirement assets dropped by approximately 20 percent.

Tellingly, such correlations have survived the great post-Lehman crash of 2008, and at times of tension in the Eurozone, they have even intensified. According to

Citigroup calculations,[2] the average correlation of S&P 500 member stocks touched 70 percent in the fall of 2011—meaning that 70 percent of a move in any given stock could be explained by the market itself, with only the remainder accounted for by the company's particular characteristics. This was a record. Over history the average correlation is far lower, at approximately 25 percent—as might be expected given the diversity of companies within the S&P.

What drove all these stocks to move together? Ultimately, it was the political news from Europe. News suggesting the euro would break up led investors to sell American and Asian stocks indiscriminately; "good" news from Europe saw them buy back into stocks. This was because the potential economic damage from Europe was so great that it swamped all traditional concerns about companies' own fortunes.

A cataclysm such as the Lehman Brothers bankruptcy in September 2008 should have shaken out the speculation from the system for a generation, but evidently it has not—and this implies that the risk of another synchronized collapse is very much alive.

One clear lesson is that in the era of globalization, it is impossible to understand the finances of any one region in isolation. Events in China and the United States, in particular, are vital for anyone trying to explain

Europe's predicament, so there are chapters both on China's remarkable revival and how it was achieved and on the U.S. policy for helping its banks muddle through the crisis. Some of these have been adapted from chapters in *The Fearful Rise* and drastically revised and updated.

There are reasons for hope. There have been no further big banking failures to follow names like Lehman Brothers or Washington Mutual into the history books. Indeed, America's banking system now appears to be its healthiest in some decades. House prices have little further to fall. The risk of disaster diminishes the longer the policy of "muddling through" continues to buy time for banks, and families, to put their houses in order.

Still, the travails of the Eurozone reveal the internal contradictions of the United States' recovery. Risks remain acute. There can be no certainty that the U.S. stock market will not fall even below its March 2009 lows before this crisis is over.

Endnotes

1. See *EMU Break-Up: Pay Now, Pay Later*, ING Bank research note written by Mark Cliffe, 1 December 2011.

2. See *Monday Morning Musings—Consulting the Correlation Quarterly*, Citigroup research note by Tobias Levkovich, 28 October 2011.

Chapter 1

Genesis of the Euro

The euro puts an end to competitive currency devalua-
tion—a scourge that has been the cause of war. The
euro creates potentially the largest capital market in
the world, encouraging investment and the creation of
employment. Welcome euro—euroff! Godspeed!
—Lord Cobbold, a U.K. foreign exchange hedge fund
manager, in a letter to the *Financial Times*, January
1999

The euro started life as an attempt to ensure
European economic integration. But the member countries had not converged enough when
the system started, with the result that a fixed common
currency perversely served to force them further apart.

"I'm OK. Euro K!" The T-shirts, distributed to employ-
ees and clients by the Dutch bank ABN Amro, caught
the mood of the moment. On January 1, 1999, after
frantic and technologically unprecedented preparations
by banks and governments across Europe, shoppers in
11 countries had a new currency. The values of a swathe

of Europe's old currencies, from the French franc and German deutschmark to the Irish punt, Portuguese escudo, Italian lira, and Spanish peseta had been forever fixed in terms of a new currency, the euro.

Others watched closely. The United Kingdom, eternally divided by debates over the European Union, stayed out. It preferred to keep the pound sterling. Greece, desperate to become the twelfth member of the Eurozone, had embarked on a fast-track privatization program, in a bid to hit the qualifications needed to join the club.

The creation of the euro was the most ambitious attempt yet to assert government control over foreign exchange markets. It promised to usher in a new order for international trade and commerce, after three decades of flux. In 1971, the post-war Bretton Woods deal, which had fixed the developed world's currencies against a U.S. dollar that was itself fixed against gold, had come to an end. Ever since, politicians had struggled to find a way to maintain control over exchange rates that were now set by markets.

Governments had announced schemes with names varying from "pegs," "snakes," and "bands" to "currency boards." All were variations on a common theme. Governments would announce a target rate for their currency—which would either be tightly pegged to another or have some flexibility—and would then intervene in the market, by buying or selling their reserves of foreign currencies, to keep to that target. But a pattern appeared: Markets would watch for currencies that were pegged at an overvalued level. This would happen when their inflation rose too far. Then, speculators would bet against the currency, and the peg would break. Sudden, sharp, and unplanned devaluations prompted by markets devastated Latin American economies such as Mexico and inflicted great harm on Korea and south-east Asia. Markets needed to be convinced that devaluation could not happen in any circumstances, and that is what Europe hoped to achieve. By doing away with their own currencies altogether, Europe's governments were showing markets their total commitment.

Most of the euro's founders, such as France's president Francois Mitterrand and German chancellor Helmut Kohl, came from a generation that could still remember the Second World War and wanted to do everything possible to bring Europe closer together. A common currency also gave Europe an economic advantage. By eliminating an important expense of cross-border trade, the members of the Eurozone had strengthened their own trading ties while making it a little harder for those outside to compete.

But ultimately, joining the euro was a vast precommitment. By joining, a country rejected the option of devaluation. And by surrendering control of monetary policy to a new European Central Bank, it also renounced the option to print money to escape a problem. The belief was that this would force countries to embark on prudent policies that would ensure longer-term growth and stability. In other words, this was a vehicle for all of Europe to enjoy an economy like Germany's.

Why go to the lengths of a single currency? Politicians had seen what happened to the euro's precursor, the European Monetary System (EMS), which operated for 14 years from 1979 until 1993. Under the EMS, Europe's currencies were allowed to vary against each other only within a fixed band.

But the governments could not simply fix their exchange rates by decree. Work remained to be done. If a country's inflation is higher, this tends to weaken their exchange rate (which after all is aimed at finding a level in which goods cost an equal amount in both countries). So to be credible, and to defend a currency peg, governments must be prepared to raise interest rates (which control inflation but also make life harder for borrowers). To maintain an exact level, they also need to have reserves of the other currency. If their commitment to fixing their exchange rate lacks credibility, and their currency is overvalued, then markets can make money by attacking it.

That was infamously revealed by Britain's enforced exit from the EMS, on Wednesday, September 16, 1992. That incident led to the collapse of the EMS and helped to convince Britons that they wanted no part of the euro when it started a few years later. It went down in British history as Black Wednesday.

British inflation was running faster than Germany's, and yet Germany maintained high interest rates. This attracted investors to park their money in Germany rather than the United Kingdom, and pushed up the value of the Deutsche Mark. Britain's pound therefore looked artificially high. Traders responded by selling pounds, putting its peg against the Deutsche Mark under greater pressure.

Black Wednesday dawned with the announcement that the Bank of England was raising its base rate from 10 to 12 percent. Since most British homeowners had variable-rate mortgages, this move implied that monthly mortgage payments would instantly rise by 20 percent—in the middle of a real estate slump. It also showed to the markets that the government was deadly serious about defending the value of the pound, which had joined the EMS two years earlier.

The pound continued to fall. At lunchtime, the Bank said it was raising rates again, to 15 percent. The government wanted the markets to believe that it was totally determined to defend the pound—even if that meant raising homeowners' borrowing costs by 50 percent in one day. Nobody believed it. The pound kept falling; and the Treasury kept trying to bolster it by using its currency reserves to buy pounds.

That night, Norman Lamont, the chancellor, announced he was "suspending" sterling's membership of the EMS exchange rate mechanism. It never rejoined. The pound dropped about 10 percent against the dollar within hours and the next day, he cut British rates down to 9 percent. What on earth had happened?

Later that month, *The Times* of London talked to George Soros, a big international investor.[1] He admitted that his funds had made a $950 million profit from the fall of the pound and as much again from other currency bets during the chaos surrounding the exchange rate mechanism.

He believed that the British could not keep the pound within the necessary range against the Deutsche Mark. The U.K. economy was in recession, and he did not see the German government helping out by lowering interest rates. He resolved to bet against the pound with such overwhelming force that it became a self-fulfilling prophecy.

He told *The Times* that he had bet $10 billion, after negotiating lines of credit with dozens of banks in advance. Taking the Bank's rise to 12 percent as the signal that sterling was about to crack, he borrowed the maximum that he could in pounds and sold them all to buy Deutsche Marks. This forced the pound down. After sterling had dropped by 10 percent, Soros converted his Marks back into pounds, and made a 10 percent profit.

After its Black Wednesday humiliation, the U.K. ironically reaped the benefits in the form of a decade-long economic expansion. The episode helped convince its politicians to stay out of the euro, which would have thwarted any chance of such a devaluation.

The EMS was disbanded after Italy also exited, and then the French franc came under attack in 1993. But this failure only intensified the resolve of the countries at the core of Europe to thwart any such speculation in future by creating a new currency. This had already been agreed at the Maastricht conference of 1991. Under the euro, with no independent currencies to attack, Soros' operation would no longer be possible. But there were still ways to bet against governments that wanted to devalue.

The Eurozone now had only one monetary policy and one currency, but each country retained control over its own fiscal policy through taxation, borrowing, and expenditure. Under the treaty that set up the euro, all would-be euro members were required to converge on certain measures including their deficits, to prevent strain on the union from fiscal policies that were too far apart.

Once within the euro, it was argued, countries' fiscal policies would have no choice but to converge. Otherwise, speculators would find an opening and the union would fail. If the U.K. had been a member of the euro in 1992, devaluation would not have been an option. But it would have continued to issue its own bonds. Governments having difficulty meeting their debts generally respond by printing money, or by devaluing their currency. Without these options, they would face default. So rather than attack its currency, henceforth traders would attack a government's debt.

Was this a realistic risk? There were at least two reasons to fear that it was. First, Europe's economies had not converged enough to be ready to sustain a common currency. They were still running at different speeds, which meant that they were not ready for a single monetary policy. As 1999 dawned, Germany's economy was growing at less than one percent per year; Spain's was rattling along at 4 percent per year (see Figure 1.1).

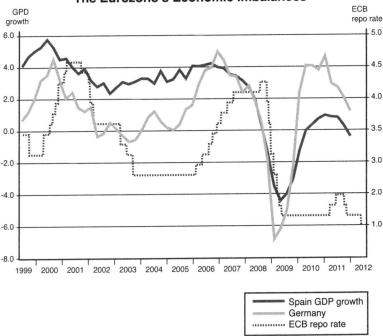

FIGURE 1.1   *From the beginning of the Eurozone, Germany and Spain were growing at very different rates, and yet they both had the same interest rate.*

What Spain needed was a few more years to prepare for convergence. If it had kept its own interest rates higher than Germany's for a while, it could have damped its economy and been ready to fall in line, without choking off its growth altogether.

Instead, and against all expectation, the single monetary policy pushed countries further apart and brought convergence to a halt. The ECB naturally set interest rates that were appropriate for Germany, its biggest member, whose economy slowed further, and spent much of the years from 2002 to 2004 in outright recession. German inflation rarely even exceeded 2 percent during this time, so the ECB therefore kept interest rates low. Spain's inflation, however, was double that of Germany (see Figure 1.2).

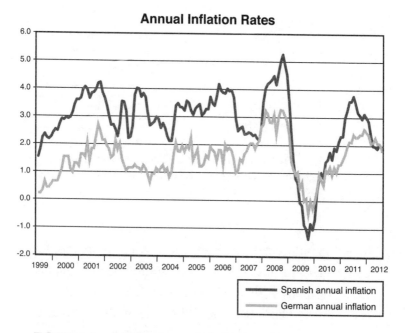

FIGURE 1.2   *Inflation was a problem in Spain, which would normally be treated with higher interest rates; but that would have created problems for Germany, which was in the doldrums.*

And so the economies diverged further. Funds from across Europe, predominantly Germany, found their way to countries like Spain, where they inflated bubbles. Spanish housing prices rocketed. That made Spanish consumers richer, creating demand for German exports and helping Germany out of its slump—at the cost of a major trade deficit for Spain, which was seriously overheating.

For another demonstration that Europe's economies had not converged enough for the straitjacket of a single currency, look at the buying power in different countries. The International Monetary Fund estimates the exchange rates needed to buy exactly the same basket of goods in two countries, known as purchasing power parity. For Germany, this level was $1 to the euro; for Spain, it was $1.45.[2] So at the advent of the euro, Spain had a wildly undervalued exchange rate. That advantage was eroded as Spain's inflation went unchecked; but it was another sign that the system had started life already out of kilter.

When Greece joined the Eurozone, two years later on January 1, 2001, the region became more unbalanced. It had rushed through a program to privatize state assets, but government spending exceeded the norm for the rest of the zone. It lacked the large manufacturing exporters of countries such as Germany and France. Within a decade the Eurozone had swollen to include

17 countries, including small island states like Malta and Cyprus and former members of the Communist bloc like Slovakia and Slovenia.

There was a second reason to fear speculative attack—Europe's banking system. In the United States, restrictive regulations had kept banks small, for decades barring them from operating outside their home state. Other rules stopped deposit-taking institutions—such as banks or savings and loans—from moving into riskier activities such as insurance and investment banking. The opposite occurred in Europe, where governments let dominant "national champion" banks take shape. Huge conglomerates with branches in all forms of financial services, they were encouraged to expand beyond their shores.[3]

The result was an unwieldy and lazy banking system, whose managers believed they had an implicit guarantee from their governments. If Europe's banks ever hit trouble, it was obvious that they were far too big to be allowed to fail. That would lead to economic disaster. But they looked as though they might also be too difficult for their home government to rescue.

As Figure 1.3 shows, in 2010, U.S. banks' assets accounted for 81 percent of American gross domestic product. The equivalent figures for Germany, France, and Spain were 294, 416, and 325 percent, respectively.

Ireland's banks, after successfully turning Dublin into a low-tax international financial center, had assets worth more than ten times the total size of the Irish economy.

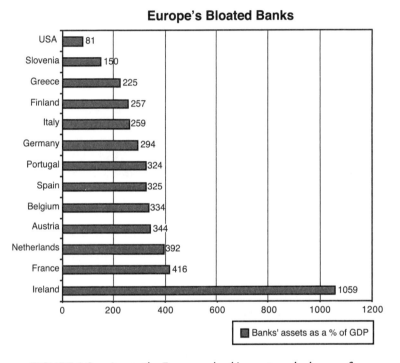

Europe's Bloated Banks

Country	Banks' assets as a % of GDP
USA	81
Slovenia	150
Greece	225
Finland	257
Italy	259
Germany	294
Portugal	324
Spain	325
Belgium	334
Austria	344
Netherlands	392
France	416
Ireland	1059

FIGURE 1.3   *Across the Eurozone, banking systems had grown far bigger than their host economies, far more bloated than that of the United States, and far too big for their governments to rescue.*

People thought little of all this as they celebrated the launch of the euro in 1999. But the seeds of disaster were already in the ground. If anything ever imperiled the banks, governments would have no choice but to help them. Then their sovereign debt would come into question; and under the euro, government debt could be attacked just as easily as George Soros had once attacked the pound sterling. All that was needed was a catalyst for trouble in the European banking system. That came 8 years later, when the U.S. banking system imploded.

Summary

The euro was set up to ensure that Europe's economies could converge with each other, but instead led to deepening imbalances.

- The euro was designed to force European economic integration and stamp out foreign exchange speculation.

- Europe's economies were not sufficiently converged at launch, with the result that a common monetary policy forced them further apart.

- Europe's bloated banks posed a risk to governments, who might not be able to bear the cost of rescuing them.

- Removing devaluation as an option meant markets could bet against government debt, rather than currencies.

- Those flaws remained hidden until the U.S. financial crisis revealed them.

Endnotes

1. See "How Mr. Soros made a billion by betting against the pound," *The Times of London*, October 26, 1992.

2. Ibid.

3. See David O. Beim. *Europe and the Financial Crisis*, Columbia Business School, March 17, 2009; http://www1.gsb.columbia.edu/mygsb/faculty/resea rch/pubfiles/3324/Europe%20and%20the%20Fina ncial%20Crisis%2Epdf. Published a year before the Eurozone crisis broke out, this paper also prophetically called on Europe to agree on a procedure to deal with requests for bailouts from individual countries.

Chapter 2

Catalyst:
Crash on Wall Street

"So I'm the schmuck?"
—Lehman Brothers Chief Executive Dick Fuld,
confronted with the news that his firm would be
forced into bankruptcy in September 2008.[1]

The Lehman Brothers bankruptcy in 2008 triggered a global crisis because the banking system had grown too interconnected. The crisis revealed that many European banks were holding on to bad U.S. debts and showed that their fate was dependent on political judgments, in both Washington and Brussels.

When Lehman Brothers sought bankruptcy protection on September 16, 2008, it was the fourth largest investment bank on Wall Street. The U.S. administration of President George W. Bush had deliberately allowed it to fail. There was no precedent for any such event, and neither bankers nor politicians had readied themselves for the consequences. Two days later, amid mounting panic, the U.S. government reversed course and promised $85 billion to help rescue the nation's biggest insurer, American International Group (AIG). A global financial panic ensued.

Many questions remained unanswered. How did Lehman fall into such a state? And why did the U.S. government decide to rescue AIG only days after it had allowed Lehman to collapse? Even though the crisis was unmistakably made in the United States, the answers to all of these questions were rooted in the Eurozone. To let AIG fail would, in all probability, have triggered the collapse of Europe's banking system.

Lehman was caught up in one of history's great investment bubbles, having bought far too much U.S. property, and also having lent to numerous parties who had no chance to repay. It had done so using borrowed money, with the result that only small falls for the investments it held could leave it insolvent. Both U.S. credit and real estate were hopelessly overpriced because of speculative bubbles that had been growing for many years. For example, house prices in Miami rose an absurd 180 percent from 2000 to 2006.[2] Mortgages to buy them were historically cheap. Individuals and investment banks alike succumbed to temptation and bought property they could not afford, for far more than it turned out to be worth.

Such bubbles inevitably recur. Markets are driven by the interplay of greed and fear, both rooted in human psychology. When greed swamps fear, as tends to happen once every generation, an irrational bubble results. When the pendulum swings back to fear, the bubble bursts, often in spectacular fashion.

History provides examples at least as far back as the 17th century Tulip Mania, in which wealthy Dutch merchants paid their lifesavings for one tulip bulb. But such insanity was a rare event. After one mania had ended, typically one or two generations would pass before another took hold.[3]

The last three decades have seen far more bubbles. Gold soared and then crashed in 1980; Mexican and other Latin American debt suffered the same fate in 1982, and again in 1994; Japanese stocks peaked and plummeted in 1990, followed soon after by Scandinavian banking stocks; stocks of the Asian Tiger economies came back to earth in 1997; and the Internet bubble burst with the Dot-Com meltdown of 2000.

True, the world had to this point enjoyed a long period of growth, including the remarkable post-war rise of Germany and Japan, the peaceful end of the Cold War, and then the rise of Asia's "tiger" economies such as South Korea and Taiwan. Maybe this was just due to understandable over-enthusiasm after a long period of prosperity.[4]

But how, then, to explain what happened next? Bubbles in U.S. house prices and in U.S. mortgage-backed bonds, which started to burst in 2006, gave way to a bubble in Chinese stocks that burst in 2007. Then 2008 saw the bursting of bubbles in oil, industrial metals, foodstuffs, Latin American stocks, Russian stocks, Indian stocks, and in currencies as varied as the Brazilian real, the British pound sterling, and the Australian dollar. As the prices of these previously unconnected and independent assets came tumbling, so Lehman—and many other investment groups that had borrowed money to invest in the bubbles—ran out of money. The investment groups' plight was made worse as their own investors struggled to pull out their money.

Rather than blame the greed of Lehman Brothers' executives for what happened, as is fashionable, it is better to ask why they, and the many other investors who created these bubbles, had apparently lost all their fear. Greed is a human constant. It is only when that greed is no longer moderated by fear that investors make disastrous mistakes like Lehman did.

My contention in *The Fearful Rise of Markets* is that over several decades, the institutionalization of investment and the spread of markets to cover more of the global economy inflated and synchronized bubbles. To recapitulate briefly, the rise of markets has brought these trends in its wake, leading to the crises in U.S. housing credit and later in European sovereign credit.

Principal/Agent Splits

In the 1950s, investment was a game for amateurs, with less than 10 percent of the stocks on the New York Stock Exchange held by institutions such as life insurance companies; now institutions drive each day's trading.[5] Although lending was once for professionals, with banks controlling virtually all decisions, that role has now been taken by the capital markets. As economists put it, in both investing and lending, the "principals" have been split from the "agents." When people make decisions about someone else's money, they tend to take riskier decisions than they would with their own money. Lehman, for example, took the risk of default on mortgages even though it had never met the homeowner. The decision to lend had been made by someone else who did not have to bear the risk of default.

Herding

The pressures on investors from the investment industry, and from their own clients, are new to this generation, and they magnify the already strong human propensity to crowd together in herds. Professional

investors have strong incentives to crowd into investments that others have already made. When the weight
of institutions' money goes to the same place at the
same time, bubbles inflate—as happened in U.S. housing and credit. When the herd turned, Lehman's share
price came under attack, making it harder for it to raise
money from the stock market, and trapping it even
more deeply. Two years later, the herd would start to
stampede through Europe's government bond markets.

Safety in Numbers

Not long ago, indexes were compiled weekly by teams
of actuaries using slide rules. Stocks, without guaranteed dividends, were considered riskier than bonds.
Now, mathematical models purport to measure risk
with precision and show how to trade risk for return.
Computers perform the necessary calculations in mil-
liseconds. The original theories were nuanced with
many caveats, but their psychological impact on
investors was cruder. They fostered the belief that markets could be understood and controlled, and that led to
overconfidence. They also promoted the idea that there
was safety in investing in different assets, or diversification. This became the orthodoxy, encouraging risk-
taking and leading investors into new markets they did
not understand. Lehman, and many European banks,

was led into subprime debt by models that wrongly suggested they were taking little or no risk.

Moral Hazard

As memories of the bank failures of the 1930s grew fainter, banks found ways around the limits imposed on them in that era, and governments eventually dismantled the limits altogether. Banks grew much bigger—in the United States, but particularly in the Eurozone. Government bank rescues made money cheaper while giving bankers the impression that there would always be a rescue if they got into trouble. That created *moral hazard*—the behavior that results when people believe they will suffer no penalty for taking undue risks. Similarly, big bonuses for short-term performance, with no risk that they would have to be paid back in the event of longer-term losses, encouraged hedge fund managers and investment bankers to take big short-term risks, further boosting overconfidence. Lehman was allowed to fail only after several other huge institutions, such as the mortgage banks Fannie Mae and Freddie Mac, or the brokerage Bear Stearns, had been rescued in bailouts coordinated by the U.S. government. Small wonder that its executives behaved as though they could not fail, and that others were so shocked when it did.

The Rise of Markets and the Fall of Banks

Financial breakthroughs turned assets once available only to specialists into tradable assets that investors anywhere in the world could buy or sell with a click of the mouse. Currencies, emerging market stocks, credit, and commodities once operated in their separate walled gardens and followed their own rules. Over the course of about two decades, they became interchangeable financial assets. When their markets expanded with the influx of money, many risky assets shot upward simultaneously, forming synchronized bubbles. Meanwhile, banks, which had specialized in many of these areas, saw their roles usurped by markets. Rather than disappear, they sought new things to do—and were increasingly lured into speculative excesses. This was particularly true of the lumbering and poorly run banks that populated the Eurozone.

All these toxic ingredients combined with a central bank over-willing to prime the pump with cheap credit to create the housing bubble in the United States. Lehman profited to the full.

But why did this create a global disaster? An analogy with the Harry Potter books might help. In *Harry Potter and the Deathly Hallows*, the schoolboy wizard discovers that the evil Voldemort has split his soul into many pieces. Nobody knows where they are. All must be found and destroyed before Voldemort can be killed. Because they are so dispersed, the assumption is that Voldemort must be indestructible. Similarly, financial institutions had dispersed and repackaged subprime assets so many times over that nobody was sure exactly who was holding on to losses. Many banks had no idea whether they themselves stood to lose.

It was an open secret on Wall Street that big European banks and pension funds had been particularly willing buyers of subprime debt. This made sense. It offered higher rates of interest than they could find at home, for what appeared to be minimal extra risk. So confidence in European banks was compromised.

That confidence was rocked further by the troubles of American International Group (AIG). It had guaranteed many of the mortgage bonds held by European banks, through complicated insurance contracts known as *credit default swaps*. Following Lehman's crash, it was evident that it did not have the money to make good on those guarantees. AIG enjoyed the top triple-A credit rating, so European banks were allowed to hold any bonds that it had insured on the assumption that they were also of top quality. They were not required to put aside capital to guard against the risk of a failure. Two days after Lehman went bankrupt, the treasury announced that it was bailing out AIG, in an operation that would eventually cost American taxpayers $182bn.

This was used to honor its credit default swaps in full—and about 80 percent of AIG's $560 billion in credit insurance had been taken out by European banks.[6] In practice, therefore, that bailout money had gone toward stopping the collapse of Europe's banks.

The authorities failed, however, to thwart a run on other banking institutions—such as money market funds. These are mutual funds that hold nothing but bank deposits and short-term bonds. Many offer checkbooks. In theory, they offer virtually the same security as an insured bank. But because they are not regulated banks and do not have to contribute toward deposit insurance, they can offer higher rates.

The proposition appeared a no-brainer. But this was a classic example of moral hazard. Knowing that their own investors assumed that the funds were riskless, the funds' managers had quietly taken on slightly greater risks to increase their profits. The Reserve Fund, the first and one of the biggest, held $785 million in Lehman Brothers bonds. When these bonds defaulted, it announced that it had taken a loss and would now pay its investors only 97 cents for each dollar invested. It had "broken the buck."

Most investors had assumed that this was impossible. So the announcement, two days after the Lehman's bankruptcy, prompted total panic. Investors pulled their money out of money market funds, forcing the funds to sell whatever they could in order to raise the cash to pay them. By week's end, the assets of institutional money market funds, investing only in government bonds, had fallen by $176 billion, whereas funds not restricted to government securities fell by $239 billion. This crippled the banks that had relied on money market funds as a key source of finance. In effect, this was a bank run.

Financiers extended loans to people with no chance of repaying them and then repackaged and dispersed those loans in such a way that nobody knew who was sitting on losses when the loans started to default. That led to a breakdown of trust in the U.S. financial system, and—because of interconnected markets—in global finance. Bad lending practices in Florida helped create a synchronized global crash.

There was another critical reason why the Lehman bust had such disastrous consequences: politics. Such serious problems went beyond the discretion of regulators or bankers, and required elected politicians to change laws and spend public money. They needed to do so swiftly, and in a way that they could justify to their voters. This introduced great uncertainty and volatility to markets. Politicians on both sides of the Atlantic also needed to prove that they could act rationally, which they signally failed to do.

In the United States, the critical issue was the Troubled Assets Relief Program (TARP), under which Treasury Secretary Hank Paulson proposed to use $700 billion of public money to inject into the banks. This measure, as we will see, ultimately proved vital in bringing the acute phase of the crisis to an end. But naturally, Congress wanted an explanation of why so much was needed and how it would be used. By September 29, 2008, after holding hearings, they appeared to have come up with a formula they could agree on, as leaders of both parties agreed to put the matter to a vote—something they would usually do only if they were confident that it would pass.

Amazingly, it was voted down. The Dow Jones Industrial Average fell 777 points, almost instantaneously, the largest ever daily fall in points terms. This wiped out some $1.5 trillion in market value, or roughly double what Congress had decided not to spend on the TARP program.

This was not an overreaction. Congress had unintentionally shown investors that they should not rely on politicians to resolve, or even pay attention, to critical financial issues. If the political institutions that frame and safeguard markets are weak and cannot be relied on, then of course investors will lose their confidence. Art Cashin, a trader who had worked on the New York Stock Exchange's floor for 47 years at the time, said it was as though the traders were on a ship in a storm—and had suddenly seen the officers and crew in a pitched battle with each other.

The Eurozone's political institutions, far younger than those of the United States and as yet untested by crisis, had no hope. The day Congress voted down the TARP, Ireland announced that it had quintupled the amount of each deposit it was prepared to cover from €20,000 to €100,000 per account. A day later it went further and said that it would insure all bank deposits. This was a startling gesture, as Ireland's banking assets far exceeded the capability of its government to guarantee them, but investors and savers elsewhere in the Eurozone knew what to do. They started to pull their funds out of local banks and entrust them to Ireland; a process that was made easy by the advent of Internet banking.

In other words, one European government had sparked a bank run for the others. Europe needed to thrash out a common approach to insurance. But the talks soon bogged down, and on Thursday of that week, Germany's Chancellor Angela Merkel said she could not and would not "issue a blank check for all banks, regardless of whether they behave in a responsible manner or not." Three days later, amid deepening panic, she announced that Germany would do exactly that, guaranteeing all deposits.

As with the TARP, the problem was not the policy so much as the unavoidable evidence that politicians could not speak with one voice. A traumatic crash in European stock markets ensued.

Although few noticed this at the time, however, the seeds of an even more traumatic crash in European bond markets had been sown. Confidence in banks had been shaken; governments had been forced to stand behind the banks; and confidence in politicians was also lost.

Summary

Lehman Brothers' collapse revealed the weakness of the European banking system, forced governments to guarantee their banks' debts, and helped push Europe into recession.

- That had the effect of weakening sovereign debt.

- Lehman's demise was catastrophic for the Eurozone because

  a. Losses were opaque and widely distributed.

  b. It caused a bank run in money market funds.

  c. It prompted a loss of confidence in politicians.

Endnotes

1. Quoted in *Too Big To Fail* by Andrew Ross Sorkin. New York: Viking, 2009.

2. This is according to the S&P Case-Shiller house price indexes. Full data for the indexes are available at: http://www.standardandpoors.com/indices/ sp-case-shiller-home-price-indices/en/us/?indexId= spusa-cashpidff--p-us----.

3. The definitive history of asset bubbles is *Manias, Panics, and Crashes,* Fifth Edition, by Charles P. Kindleberger and Robert Aliber. Hoboken: Wiley, 2005.

4. The market historians Elroy Dimson, Paul Marsh, and Mike Staunton refer to the second half of the 20th century as "the triumph of the optimists." See *Triumph of the Optimists* by Elroy Dimson, Paul Marsh, and Mike Staunton. Princeton: Princeton University Press, 2001.

5. These figures are maintained by the Federal Reserve.

6. David O. Beim. *Europe and the Financial Crisis* by
    Columbia Business School, March 17, 2009;
    http://www1.gsb.columbia.edu/mygsb/faculty/
    research/pubfiles/3324/Europe%20and%20the%
    20Financial%20Crisis%2Epdf. Published a year
    before the Eurozone crisis broke out, this paper also
    prophetically called on Europe to agree on a proce-
    dure to deal with requests for bailouts from
    individual countries.

Chapter 3

Emerging Markets
Decouple

*The Great Wall [of China] is evidence of a historical
inability of people in this part of the planet to
communicate, to confer and jointly determine how
best to deploy enormous reserves of human energy
and intellect.[1]*

—Ryszard Kapuscinski

The recovery started in emerging markets, which no longer followed developed markets' lead. The good news is that the bigger emerging markets have indeed "emerged," with strong institutions; the bad news is that unsustainably cheap money in China was needed for the recovery.

After Lehman, concern at first shifted not to Europe, but to the emerging markets. Everything seemed set for a replay of the disasters of the 1990s, when sudden exits of international money had led first to a currency crisis and then a debt crisis in countries from Mexico and Brazil to Thailand and South Korea. Government defaults seemed a real possibility; but they did not

43

happen. Instead, emerging markets led the world in a rebound. That helped Europe climb out of its own recession. It also showed how the Eurozone could avoid a crisis of its own—but those lessons were not followed.

Foreign exchange markets were central to the problem. Post-Lehman, American investors desperately sold international investments to bring their money home. That pushed up the dollar against other currencies. That nearly precipitated disaster. Why?

Look at Korea, where companies bought Knock-In Knock-Out options, known as Kiko options, to hedge against swings in the exchange rate. These options "knocked in" to protect against a rise in the local currency up to a certain point, when they would "knock out." That meant that there was a limit on their protection against a big rise or fall. For years before Lehman, the dollar had steadily weakened against the Korean won, so companies buying these options from banks had successfully bet that their currency would keep rising. But if the won dropped below the rate at which the contracts knocked "in," then the companies were on the hook to compensate the banks who sold them the options. Companies had effectively let the banks place a bet with them that their currency would fall.

Once the won fell, those bets went bad, and some 571 small- and medium-sized companies lost money. [2] The spread of the problem showed how indiscriminately banks had sold the options. Companies in Mexico, Brazil, Hong Kong, India, Indonesia, Malaysia, Poland, and Taiwan suffered similar losses from currency options. According to the International Monetary Fund, as many as 50,000 emerging markets companies lost money, including 10 percent of Indonesia's exporters. Losses in Brazil were $28 billion, according to the IMF, whereas in Indonesia they were $3 billion. Mexico, whose third-largest retailer, Comercial Mexicana, filed for bankruptcy, and Poland suffered losses of $5 billion each. Sri Lanka's publicly owned Ceylon Petroleum Company lost $600 million, and even the huge Chinese bank Citic Pacific lost $2.4 billion.

Regulators watched foreign exchange (forex) positions at banks closely, but they did not keep the same watchful eye on nonfinancial companies such as supermarkets or television manufacturers. That omission nearly turned a crisis into a disaster.

Money flowed out of emerging markets, pushing their currencies down further, in response to the panic in the west. As securities in countries like Brazil and Russia had been at unsustainably high bubble prices only months earlier, many foreigners were still sitting on profits, making them all the more anxious to sell. As they sold bonds, lowering their price, so their yields rose, making it more expensive for companies, or governments, to borrow.

When companies ran into forex losses, they had to buy dollars, pushing their own currencies down further. It is the possibility of just such a spiral in the Eurozone that now provokes so much concern.

This painful cycle was the exact opposite of *decoupling*, the popular theory that emerging markets were no longer dependent on the developed world for their growth, and therefore offered a hedge against problems in the United States or Europe. Far from offering such protection, emerging markets dropped by two-thirds, according to MSCI indexes, in the 12 months after their peak on Halloween, 2007. In doing so, they underperformed the developed world, where the roots of their problem lay, by 26 percent.

Fragile systems were tested for the first time and in some cases failed. Russia had to close its two biggest stock exchanges for several days in September under the weight of orders. The momentum seemed unstoppable.

But on October 27, 2008, that momentum halted. Emerging markets' stocks stopped falling, wobbled, and then began a rally, even as fresh panics over the banks saw the developed world markets fall to even worse lows. Figure 3.1 shows this reversed a longstanding pattern; the emerging markets had at last decoupled. They hit bottom and started to recover before anyone in the developed world. The importance of this cannot be overstated; after a generation in which they had offered a more extreme version of conditions in the developed world, doing better when times were good and worse when times were bad, markets in the two regions had parted company.

Emerging Markets Decouple

FIGURE 3.1   *For a decade, emerging markets simply acted like an exaggerated version of the developed markets. Then in the fall of 2008, when China announced a new stimulus program, they suddenly parted company.*

What happened? First, the developed world came up with aid. U.S. policymakers knew that big emerging market defaults would ensure a Depression. So on October 30, the Federal Reserve announced "swap lines" of $30 billion each for the central banks of Brazil, Mexico, Singapore, and South Korea.[3] In English, this meant that they lent dollars to these countries' central banks, which could in turn be lent to domestic companies desperate to pay off dollar-denominated loans. Crucially, the central banks could do this without buying dollars on the open market, which would have pushed the local currencies down further. Trying to avoid moral hazard, the Fed restricted its aid to well-managed countries whose stability was crucial to the financial system. It adroitly headed off the dynamic by which currency devaluations had turned into debt crises in the past.

But most important, in late October news filtered out that China had a stimulus plan. China was sitting on a huge war chest in the form of its foreign reserves. Unlike western governments, it could afford to jump-start its economy.

Chinese economic data is carefully managed, but the figures that are hardest to massage looked alarming. For example, electricity generation was falling, implying that the economy might be contracting. Factories making cheap toys and shoes in the Pearl River Delta near

Hong Kong shut suddenly amid complaints from workers that factory owners had absconded without paying wages.

At the least, there was a danger that China's annual growth would drop below 6 percent for the first time since the 1989 violent clamp down on pro-democracy activists in Tiananmen Square. Sluggish growth would have violated the Communist Party's longstanding compact with the people, who were denied democracy, but assured of strong economic growth in return.[4]

The hope was that China would reply with devastating force to boost its economy. It did.

The stimulus package, when announced in October 2008, came to $586 billion (for a headline number of 4 trillion renminbi) of new government spending in two years on infrastructure and social welfare projects.[5] It sounded like a New Deal. This was part of an "active" fiscal policy, whereas monetary policy would be "moderately active," according to official party pronouncements. Relief was palpable. The Shanghai Composite rose 7.3 percent that day and then doubled over the next nine months. And commodities lurched to news from China, the greatest user of metals. Copper rose 10 percent in a day.

The final reason why emerging markets turned around is that they had learned the lessons from the crises of the

1980s and 1990s, unlike the United States and Western Europe. When the Kiko options debacle briefly threatened a new crisis, emerging markets showed they were no longer as vulnerable to the flows of international capital. "Markets behaved the way they always do, which is that they misbehaved. They reached the ledge," said Antoine van Agtmael, who had invented emerging markets as an asset class a quarter of a century earlier. "And then people said: 'This is ridiculous.'"

He used a medical analogy. "Pandemics are dangerous when the immune system is poor. But pandemics are mitigated if the immune system is good. Basically the emerging markets had better immune systems than most people thought."[6] In other words, they had foreign reserves, their consumers had little debt, and their banks were well regulated.

Nations besides China had stockpiled foreign reserves to fend off currency swings. Russia spent $200 billion in an (unsuccessful) attempt to defend the ruble. South Korea was sitting on $240 billion—compared to $22 billion when its crisis hit in 1997.

Furthermore, emerging markets' stocks were relatively cheap, while developed world governments were printing cash that allowed investors to buy them. By the end of November 2009, $72.5 billion had flowed into emerging market funds, far exceeding the previous record of $54 billion for the bubble year of 2007. That drove an epic rally. A year after hitting bottom, the emerging markets index had more than doubled, with the Brics (Brazil, Russia, India and China—the four biggest economies and investment destinations in the emerging world) up 145 percent. The strongest stock market in the world over that time, gaining 195 percent, was Peru—a big exporter of metals to China.

China's metals imports were so prodigious that it was hard to see how they could all be used. Its copper imports doubled in the first nine months of the year, causing the global copper price to double.[7] Much of this appeared to be stockpiling, or speculation, but it was still enough to drive revivals for Peru and other commodity-exporting countries—and also, to a lesser extent, the Eurozone, where many manufacturers served the Chinese market.

The markets' logic was self-reinforcing. But at its heart lay a Chinese recovery that seemed self-contradictory. How could it administer such a drastic stimulus without having to withdraw it later? And how could China take such action without serious and negative consequences for other countries?[8] As it turned out, despite its initial help in enabling European economies to claw back from disaster in 2009, China's desperation tactics would soon help to force Europe into crisis.

Summary

In 2008, China and other emerging markets nearly fell into a financial crisis to match the crisis that hit the Eurozone a few years later, but averted it by printing money and spending it.

- Emerging markets avoided crisis thanks to:

    1. Strong political and economic institutions, which had matured since the 1980s and 1990s.

    2. Aid from the Federal Reserve to thwart a currency crisis.

    3. Aggressively expansionary fiscal policy by China.

    4. Cheap monetary policies, both in emerging markets and in the United States.

- The Eurozone had none of these factors when dealing with its own crisis.

- Emerging markets' resurgence helped Europe and the United States weather their own recessions.

Endnotes

1. See *Travels with Herodotus* by Ryszard Kapuscinski. New York: Vintage International, 2008.

2. See "Playing with Fire" by Randall Dodd. *Finance & Development*, June 2009, Volume 46, Number 2. Published by the IMF.

3. See "Fed supports emerging economies" by Krishna Guha. *Financial Times*, October 30, 2008.

4. See "Slowdown forces rethink on social compact" by Tom Mitchell. *Financial Times*, November 10, 2008.

5. See "China authorises 'massive' stimulus package" by Geoff Dyer. *Financial Times*, November 9, 2008.

6. Conversation with the author in New York City, October 6, 2009.

7. See "A copper kettle mania in China has boiled up for a bull market" by John Dizard. *Financial Times*, November 14, 2009.

8. See "Short View: China's Bubble" by John Authers. *Financial Times*, August 12, 2009.

Chapter 4

Currency Wars

We're in the midst of an international currency war, a general weakening of currency. This threatens us because it takes away our competitiveness.
—Guido Mantega, Brazilian finance minister, September 27, 2010

Low rates and weak currencies in China and the United States pushed money toward other emerging countries and kept the euro unnaturally strong. That exported inflation to the emerging world, and left Europe uncompetitive.

In November 2008, China announced a "moderately active" monetary policy that soon turned out to be hyperactive. State-controlled banks tripled new lending in the first half of 2009, compared to the first half of 2008—an explosion in credit almost certain to create overheating. The Chinese authorities soon tried to rein it in.

Indeed, China was so big that its lending boom not only overheated its own domestic economy, but it also had a critical impact on Europe, most painfully in the currency market. China might even have held the answer to a persistent mystery of the Eurozone crisis—why the euro remained strong, even as its very existence was called into question. This was damaging as a weaker euro might have helped countries like Spain to improve their trade balances.

As China's huge foreign currency reserves rise, it diversifies its holdings by selling dollars and buying euros. That strengthens the euro. When Simon Derrick of BNY Mellon mapped Chinese reserve accumulation against the euro, the pattern was clear: The euro strengthened whenever China was building reserves (see Figure 4.1). This even happened in late 2011 when the political crisis in the Eurozone's crisis toppled elected governments in Italy and Greece. The euro remarkably spent two years above the low it set in the summer of 2010, when the crisis seemed far less severe than it eventually became. It is unlikely to be a coincidence that China was allowing reserves to decline in 2010, and that it resumed its build-up of reserves over the next two years, as Europe's woes deepened, and the euro rose.

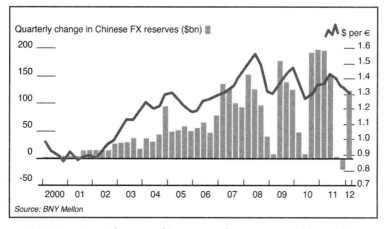

FIGURE 4.1   *Whenever China acquired new reserves of U.S. dollars, it would sell some of them and buy euros. That appears to have pushed the euro up against the dollar when it might otherwise have weakened.*

Much of China's newly created money went into real estate, where it appeared to form bubbles even greater than the one that had formed in the United States a few years earlier. In 2010, a record 70 percent of China's gross domestic product went on so-called "fixed-asset investment"—mostly infrastructure and real estate. For comparison, during the U.K. and U.S. property bubbles a few years earlier, such investment peaked at less than 20 percent of GDP.

Meanwhile, satellite images and crusading journalism revealed freshly built cities standing empty across China. Perhaps the most famous was Ordos in Inner

Mongolia, where a new district designed to house a million people remained empty five years after it had been built.[1] Whether through deliberate corruption or incompetence, excessive supplies of cheap credit had a predictable effect and spurred misallocation of capital on a massive scale.

Furthermore, inflation—a big political issue in China—took flight. In 2010, China tried to end the stimulus by hiking interest rates and tightening banks' reserve requirements. That turned global sentiment against emerging markets *en masse*. China started easing once more in late 2011, raising hopes that it had done the near-impossible and deflated a bubble without bursting it. But many still doubted.

Those doubts showed up most clearly in the Chinese stock market. The rally in Shanghai stocks ended in August 2009. After that, they steadily lost one-third of their value, drastically underperforming the world's other big markets. Industrial metals prices also dropped. From 2008 to 2011, stock markets in the Bric countries of Brazil, Russia, India, and China significantly underperformed the S&P 500, the main benchmark of the United States. And Chinese fears reverberated around the world.

International stocks, particularly in Europe, sold off in the summer and fall of 2011. The Eurozone crisis and U.S. political wrangles were producing ample reasons for concern. But a Deutsche Bank study of the biggest European stocks found that companies making most of their profits in the U.S. dropped only 9 percent in the worst 12 months of that sell-off. By contrast, stocks of companies focused on China fell by as much as 50 percent at one point[2] (see Figure 4.2) China has acted as a crucial counterweight to problems in Europe. It no longer had that effect, even as the Chinese economy continued to grow. This implied that a true Chinese crisis could easily turn into disaster in the Eurozone.

The effects went beyond the Eurozone. During the previous emerging markets bubble, which burst in the summer of 2008, the Chinese currency gradually rose against the dollar, making life harder for Chinese exporters. The renminbi rose by approximately 20 percent in three years. But during the emerging markets rally of 2009, China's currency stayed pegged to the dollar, so flows of dollars into countries like Brazil forced up the local currency against both the dollar and the renminbi. In the United States, the Federal Reserve, under Ben Bernanke, was aggressively pushing down interest rates, which should have directly weakened the dollar. Instead, it made both the United States *and* China more competitive because their currencies moved together. When China let its currency start gaining once more in the summer of 2010, it rose only one-half as fast as it had during the managed appreciation that had ended in 2008.

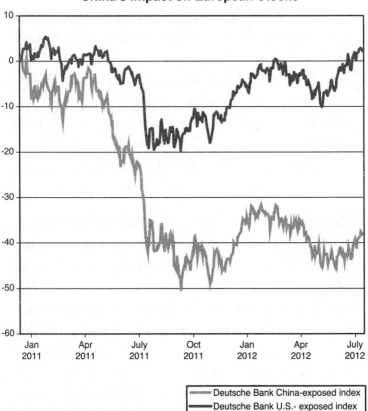

China's Impact on European Stocks

Deutsche Bank China-exposed index
Deutsche Bank U.S.- exposed index

FIGURE 4.2   *Worries about China and its imports showed up most clearly in the European stock market. During 2011 and 2012, European stocks exposed to China fell terribly, but the stocks most exposed to the United States managed to hold their ground.*

Currency traders amplified the weakness of the dollar and renminbi by sending money wherever it could earn a higher yield, such as Brazil, whose interest rates were anchored in double figures. That pumped up the prices of Brazil's stocks and real estate, risking overheating those markets and forcing up the Brazilian currency. The influx of funds meant higher inflation, which the central bank fought with higher interest rates—which in turn encouraged more funds into the country and pushed up the Brazilian real still further, while slowing the economy. Brazil's real gained 60 percent against the dollar from its 2008 crisis low until its summer 2011 peak. That in turn made Brazil's exporters ever less competitive, provoking the ire of its politicians.

In 2010, Guido Mantega, Brazil's finance minister, complained of an "international currency war."[3] Brazil had already attempted to curb the inflows in 2008 by taxing incoming investments in stocks or bonds—a clear sign that the foreign cash was now unwelcome. Several Asian countries now took similar measures. Turkey, wracked by similar problems, resorted to cutting rates to try to control inflation. The opposite of conventional economics, the argument was that making money cheaper would dampen the flows of foreign money that were sparking inflation in the country. Such logic made sense in a world where the inter-connectedness of markets had swamped traditional economic assumptions.

Overvalued currencies were not limited to emerging markets. The Swiss franc has long been regarded as a strong currency, with persistent high interest rates and low inflation. In the teeth of the crisis, that led to crazy exchange rates. In March 2009, just as stock markets were hitting bottom, the Swiss National Bank announced it was selling its own currency to keep its exchange rate below 1.50 to the euro. That worked for a while, but as anxieties about Europe deepened in 2011, traders rushed back into the franc. That forced it much higher, to 1.10 to the euro. This hurt large Swiss exporters like Novartis and Nestlé, as it reduced the value of international sales in Swiss francs.[4] Eventually, the SNB had no choice but to intervene to hold the franc to a minimum of 1.20 against the euro. Despite the troubled history of such pegs, Switzerland had the reserves and the credibility to make it stick, and this rate held for six months.

There were similar distortions in the rate against the U.S. dollar. At one point in 2011, only 0.72 Swiss francs were needed to buy a dollar; but it actually took 1.68 Swiss francs to buy an equal amount of goods as $1, according to the International Monetary Fund.

Such currency swings made life difficult for a mature economy like Switzerland's; they were even harder for emerging markets. And as emerging markets provided a critical source of growth for the Eurozone (whether in eastern Europe, a center for German manufacturers, or in Latin America, a popular destination for Spain's international conglomerates), it also made life difficult for Europe.

The greater problem remained China. It had come to the rescue in 2008, but it grew clearer that it could not or would not do the same thing again in 2012 (see Figure 4.3). By that summer, import growth had ground almost to a halt, factory production was poor, and China cut its official growth target to 7.5 percent, the slowest in 13 years.

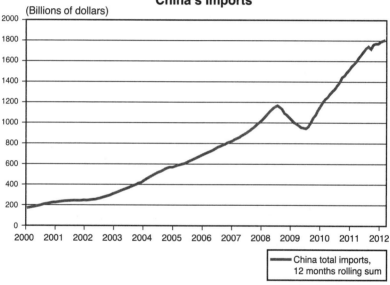

China's Imports

(Billions of dollars)

China total imports, 12 months rolling sum

FIGURE 4.3   *For more than a decade, the rest of the world accustomed itself to steadily rising Chinese imports. By 2012, it looked as though such growth could no longer be taken for granted.*

The Chinese Communist Party, preparing for a leadership change at the end of the year, also laid the groundwork for a new policy. In May 2012, Xinhua, its official news agency, announced, "It will not unveil another massive stimulus plan to stimulate economic growth. Current policies to stabilize growth will not repeat the old way of stimulating growth three years ago."[5]

Instead of sucking money into imports and property bubbles, as in 2008, China would focus on building domestic infrastructure and building demand at home. This would lead to more balanced and equitable growth. But both the United States and Europe had been hoping to sell China more exports. This time, Chinese money would not be available to bail out Europe from a crisis.

Summary

China was an essential driver of Europe's problems, first keeping the euro too strong, and then undermining European exporters.

- By accumulating foreign exchange reserves and moving some of them into euros, China made it harder for the euro to fall against the dollar.

- By tying its currency to the dollar, China exported inflation to other emerging markets, making them less competitive and forcing them to slow their economies.

- China's economic policy is shifting toward promoting internal growth, not imports from other countries; that could remove Europe's major source of external growth.

Endnotes

1. See "Ordos, China: A Modern Ghost Town, photo essay" by Michael Christopher Brown. Time; http://www.time.com/time/photogallery/0,29307,1975397_2094492,00.html.

2. See "European Equity Strategy: Europe's Globally Exposed" by Gareth Evans research note published by Deutsche Bank, October 10, 2011.

3. See "Brazil in 'Currency War' Alert" by Jonathan Wheatley and Peter Garnham. *Financial Times*, September 27, 2010.

4. See "Nestlé: Unpopular Decisions Required," The Lex Column. *Financial Times*, August 10, 2011.

5. See "China Stimulus Unnecessary, Risks Further Damage" by Nick Edwards and Kevin Yao. Reuters, May 30, 2012. http://www.reuters.com/article/2012/05/30/us-china-economy-stimulus-idUSBRE84T06U20120530

Chapter 5

Banks Bounce

After a crash has occurred, it is important to wait long enough for the insolvent firms to fail, but not so long as to let the crisis spread to the solvent firms that need liquidity—"delaying the death of the strong swimmers."[1]

—Charles P. Kindleberger, economic historian

W orld markets recovered only after investors grew confident that no more big U.S. banks would fail or be nationalized. That started a "positive feedback" loop, as confidence made financing easier to obtain. Governments won that confidence by treating banks with exceptional generosity.

The news that turned around the U.S. and European markets came in an internal memo. From October 2008 to March 2009, Citigroup took four separate bailouts from the U.S. government to stay afloat, and its share price dipped below $1. Formal nationalization seemed inevitable. Vikram Pandit, Citi's CEO, wanted to reassure his 300,000 employees, so he told them that "we were profitable through the first two months of 2009 and are having our best quarter-to-date performance since the third quarter of 2007." He also said that deposits were "relatively sound," suggesting that there was no bank run despite the bad publicity.[2]

Along with the boost from the Chinese economy, confidence that U.S. banks could survive intact became the second pillar of one of history's greatest stock market rallies. But such confidence did not extend to the Eurozone, whose banks were arguably even more vulnerable because they had grown so big. Over the ensuing months, the U.S. government steadily took measures needed to bolster confidence in the country's banks. Eurozone authorities failed to take such action, and that would come back to haunt them.

On the day of Mr. Pandit's memo, Citi's share price rose almost 40 percent, while the S&P grew 6.5 percent.[3] The effect on European banks and their share prices was almost as marked. Just as an analyst's warning on Citi had brought world stock markets down from their peak on Halloween 2007, so it was more news from Citi that marked the bottom 16 months later.

It had such an impact for two reasons. First, as at any market bottom, fear swamped greed. As Citi became a penny stock, the S&P 500 touched the ominous number of 666, erasing its gains since August 1996. Surveys suggested investor confidence had never been lower. The weekly survey of the American Association of Individual Investors found 70 percent of its respondents feeling bearish—the highest on record and more pessimistic than in the desperate weeks after the Lehman collapse. In such conditions, it needs only a minor news item, like an unaudited, non-legally binding internal memo, to turn confidence around.

Second, central banks had surgically stripped the fear from the markets on which banks depend. Government cash had brought investors back into commercial paper, mortgages, and corporate credit. That created cheaper financing and favorable conditions for banks. For shareholders there remained the risk that nationalization would wipe them out, but Pandit's memo, showing that Citi was making money again, turned around sentiment on this score. The belief that a government takeover had been averted sent money back into the stock market.

In sum, although obscured behind an alphabet soup of acronyms, the government's clear message was that it would let no major bank fail. That message created a positive feedback loop. Confidence in one market altered the reality of other markets and let them recover.

The government's package unrolled bit by bit in the days after the October 2008 crash. First, the Federal

Reserve directly bought commercial paper—short-term bonds issued by companies—to finance items like payroll. This meant that it had entered the business of lending to companies that were not banks, a huge extension of its remit.[4] This signaled that it was safe to buy commercial paper again, making it much easier for banks themselves, which issued a lot of commercial paper, to raise funds.

The United States also sharply increased the maximum deposits it was prepared to insure from $100,000 to $250,000. For many, this removed the incentive to pull money out of their accounts, and headed off continued runs on U.S. banks. The American authorities also took the drastic step of guaranteeing all money market funds outright, quelling the run on these funds. Not all jurisdictions took such emphatic action. In most Eurozone countries, deposit insurance remained capped at €100,000, roughly half the U.S. level.

Then, Britain's premier Gordon Brown announced a £400 billion bank bailout. This was almost as much as the $700 billion that the U.S. Congress voted for the highly contentious Troubled Asset Relief Program (TARP), even though the U.K. is less than one-fifth the size of the U.S. Britain used the money to buy stakes in troubled banks, a form of nationalization, but surprisingly the market liked the move. That prompted the

U.S. Treasury, at that point controlled by Hank Paulson under President George W. Bush, to do the same.

Mr. Paulson bought direct stakes in big banks, regardless of whether they wanted the money. This raised banks' capital so that they could afford to take more losses. He followed up with targeted rescues for big banks that got into trouble: Citigroup took an extra $20 billion in capital from the government, along with guarantees for a stunning $300 billion of its most problematic debt-backed securities;[5] Bank of America also received $20 billion, along with guarantees of $118 billion of debt.[6] The two behemoth banks created by a string of mergers a decade earlier were, indeed, too big to fail—and this action was a relief for the markets. The Eurozone, where each country retained responsibility for its own banks, in general avoided forced recapitalizations. That left European banks looking weaker, sowing the seeds for a crisis once their loans were called into question.

Next, there was the TALF, or term asset-backed securities loan facility, in which the Fed offered to lend up to $200 billion to holders of student loans, auto loans, credit card loans, and small business loans. These were all forms of credit that were not yet deep in trouble, but where the panic might soon spread. This erected a firewall around the problem.

The Fed also said that it would spend up to $600 billion buying mortgage bonds issued or guaranteed by quasi-governmental agencies such as Fannie Mae and Freddie Mac. This enabled banks to sell the more "toxic" securities on their balance sheet. It also persuaded some speculators to try buying them at cheap prices in the hope of selling them to the government. This brought life back to the mortgage market.

In March 2009 came quantitative easing (QE), the jargon for a central bank buying government bonds to push prices up and yields down—a form of printing money. Central banks hate doing this, as it is directly inflationary. Thus this showed utter determination by the Fed to keep banks from collapsing. When the economy slowed again in the summer 2010, Ben Bernanke and the Fed were there again with "QE2," which buoyed share prices again. In Britain, the Bank of England was more aggressive with three separate doses of QE; the European Central Bank, far more concerned by inflation, largely eschewed the tactic (see Figure 5.1).

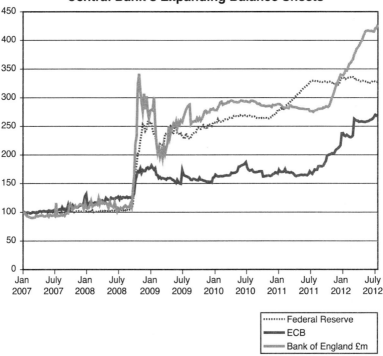

FIGURE 5.1   *Starting with the credit crunch that began in 2007, the Federal Reserve and the Bank of England both aggressively expanded their balance sheets, buying bonds and loans to help out the banks. The European Central Bank was far less aggressive.*

In April 2009, the United States even allowed banks to fudge their accounts. Under "fair value" accounting, banks had to value their assets at the price they could currently fetch in the market. They complained that in the event of a panic, this would force an irrational markdown that could render them insolvent. The new rules, rushed through by the main U.S. accounting standards body amid claims from big investor groups that they had succumbed to political pressure, gave banks more flexibility. Rather than see the value of their assets plummet with the market, they could now simply assume a higher price.

All these measures sound like desperation. They were. But their effect on investors is best understood using game theory. Politicians were daring them to take risks. There was no money to be made by making secure investments because interest rates were zero. Bond yields were not going to rise because the government would not let them. The government was not going to allow another Lehman either. Moral hazard was back— if a big bank took one risk too many, it would be rescued. That made the calculus in favor of taking a risk irresistible.

Now, consider the games that individual fund managers play against each other. Staying in cash paid them nothing; their peers, against whom they were judged, made big profits as markets recovered; and so the pressure to start buying riskier assets was overwhelming, even for those who believed the government's desperation tactics would end badly. The herding instinct was made stronger as confidence returned to different markets. Activity returned to commercial paper markets and then to mortgages and good-quality credit. That relieved the pressure on banks—even when the economy was still in free fall—so investors started buying stock.

Having embarked on this strategy, governments then had to play for time to ensure no further panic before confidence could take hold in markets. In the United States, the Obama administration did this by taking months to carry out "stress tests"—computer simulations to see how the big banks would fare in the event of bad economic downturns. Many complained that they were barely even "stress" tests as the scenarios they tested were far from the worst imaginable, but the wait for the results—which were leaked in advance—helped to take heat out of the situation.[7]

When the stress test results appeared, they showed that ten big banks had to raise an extra $75 billion in capital. Months earlier, this would have been impossible, but with markets riding higher on hopes of a China-centric global recovery, banks found buyers quickly, proving that confidence was returning.

European banking appeared to give much greater reason for concern. At the end of 2007, on the eve of the crisis, U.S. banks had total leverage of 12.2 times their equity—in other words, their total loans, on which they hoped to earn money, were worth 12.2 times the value of the equity in the company that belonged to share-holders. Any reductions in their assets (through written off loans) would reduce that equity. This might sound over-levered, but U.S. banks were far more conservative than their European counterparts. Germany's banks had leverage of 42 times their equity, while France stood at 36.[8] Europe's distended banking system needed far bigger re-capitalizations to bolster their equity than the American banks.

And yet when European banking supervisors conducted their own stress tests, a year later, they had less impact. Of 91 banks tested, only 7 failed. All the failures were either in Greece, already in crisis, or among smaller banks in Spain.[9] And if some questioned whether the United States had actually tested for the worst possible stress, the European tests were shown to be utterly inadequate less than two years later. For example, European banks were tested to see whether they could endure a write-down of 23.1 percent on the Greek bonds they held—and in February 2012, Greek bondholders were required to take a hit of 53.5 percent, more than double that. Therefore, European regulators' stress tests failed to bolster their banks in the way that the U.S. exercise had done.

Nevertheless, when the U.S. banks' capital was in place, investors on both sides of the Atlantic breathed more freely. Both a general banking collapse and a forced nationalization had been prevented. But with those risks now off the table, the question of how to avert another crisis remained. That proved much harder.

Summary

Europe failed to match the U.S. government's actions after the Lehman collapse and act decisively to bolster confidence in its banks.

- The U.S. policy avoided the nationalizations that had been expected. It rested on four pillars:

  1. Forced recapitalizations to give the banks a greater buffer against losses

  2. Stress tests to show whether they could survive a crisis or recession

  3. Stronger deposit insurance

  4. Very cheap money from the Federal Reserve

- Banks still rely to a great extent on moral hazard.

- Europe left itself open to another banking crisis by failing to act as radically on any of these four points.

Endnotes

1. *Manias, Panics, and Crashes,* Fifth Edition, by Charles P. Kindleberger and Robert Aliber. Hoboken: Wiley, 2005, p. 241. Kindleberger was quoting J.H. Clapham, the historian of the Bank of England.

2. See "Citi has strong start to the year" by Francesco Guerrera. *Financial Times*, March 10, 2009.

3. See "Citigroup helps lift markets worldwide" by Francesco Guerrera and Michael MacKenzie. *Financial Times*, March 11, 2009.

4. The New York Fed explained why it took this action at http://www.newyorkfed.org/markets/cpff_faq.html

5. See "US agrees bail-out for Citigroup" by Greg Farrell and Henny Sender in New York and Andrew Ward. *Financial Times*, November 24, 2008.

6. See "Bank of America gets $138bn lifeline" by Sundeep Tucker. *Financial Times*, January 15, 2009.

7. See "Stress tests show $75bn buffer needed" by Krishna Guha in Washington and Francesco Guerrera and Alan Rappeport in New York. *Financial Times*, May 7, 2009.

8. All these figures are drawn from David Beim, *Europe and the Financial Crisis*, by David O. Beim. Columbia Business School, March 17, 2009.

9. See "European bank stress tests," The Lex Column, *Financial Times*, July 23, 2010.

Chapter 6

Bank-Bashing

The first thing you need to know about Goldman Sachs is that it's everywhere. The world's most powerful investment bank is a great vampire squid wrapped around the face of humanity, relentlessly jamming its blood funnel into anything that smells like money.
—Matt Taibbi, *Rolling Stone*, April 5, 2010

L etting banks "muddle through" provoked political hostility; and new injections of money for the banks proved necessary to keep the market rally going.

Only one big investment bank weathered the crisis with its reputation more or less intact: Goldman Sachs. Wall Street's most prestigious institution had guarded against the risks of a collapse in housing prices, making repeated big bets against the price of subprime securities. With the most intense phase of the crisis evidently over by the end of 2009, and many competitors gone, it should have been time for Goldman to make money again as it had always done.

But, it was not. Instead, Goldman's reputation was about to go through the mincer. Its travails showed that the banking system, in the United States and in Europe, remained weak, shaking investors' confidence—particularly in the Eurozone. The problem in the short term was that "muddling through" with cheap public money tended to boost banks' profits. This was unpopular with voters, but politicians needed banks to make those profits to shore up their balance sheets. For the longer term, it was vital to impose new regulations that would make the banking system safer—and in the process inevitably make banks far less profitable. Banks, emboldened by the obvious fact that governments could not allow them to fail, fought back. Politicians, fearful of tipping banks back into crisis, backed off. Problems went uncorrected. It was an ugly political dynamic. And as the public watched what the relatively "good" banks had done to stay out of trouble, they did not like what they saw.

Goldman moved to the eye of the storm in April 2010 when *Rolling Stone* magazine branded it a "vampire squid" in a cover piece. The grotesque image stuck—particularly on trading floors, where the bank started to be known as Goldman Squids. Days later, the Securities and Exchange Commission sued Goldman for fraud. With plenty of internal e-mails to back them up, the commission alleged that Goldman had set up a mortgage-backed security that was meant to fail.

Despite initial appearances, the case was central to the difficulties of the European banking system. It revolved around a "synthetic collateralized debt obligation,"[1] known as *Abacus*. This is how it worked. First, mortgage lenders made loans to subprime borrowers with poor credit histories. Those loans were packaged up in mortgage-backed bonds. Then those bonds, with others, were used to back bundles of bonds known as collateralized debt obligations (CDOs), which were then sold to investors.

Then Goldman put together a list of different mortgage-backed bonds to create a synthetic CDO. The word "synthetic" meant that it was not directly backed by any mortgages. Instead, Goldman created a credit default swap, a form of insurance policy. In essence, a first "short" investor agreed to pay the interest payments generated by the chosen mortgage-backed bonds to a second "long" investor. In return, the "long" investor undertook to make the "short" investor whole if and when the underlying CDO defaulted (in other words, when poor Americans could no longer keep up payments on houses they could not afford).[2]

Nobody in the "real world" of housing finance had received any money. Put one way, Abacus, pieced together by Goldman Sachs, let the long investors "synthetically" copy the experience of buying a CDO—they would receive the payments if the investment survived and would bear the costs if it defaulted, just as if they actually owned it. Put another way, Goldman had acted as a bookie, bringing together clients who wanted to bet that this particular group of subprime CDOs would default, and another bunch of clients ready to bet that it would not.

The case was important because the two main suckers betting that everything would be alright included IKB, a German bank, and the U.K.'s Royal Bank of Scotland. Both were among the first financial institutions to run into trouble as the crisis took hold in 2007 and needed bailouts from their governments. This was quite typical; it was an open secret on Wall Street that big, generally poorly run European banks were the easiest targets when it came to selling questionable investments. Such products were critical in transporting the American banking crisis across the Atlantic.

Meanwhile the "short" investor was the hedge fund manager John Paulson, who became a billionaire several times over by correctly betting that subprime credit would crash. His success was even feted in a popular book called *The Greatest Trade Ever* by Gregory Zuckerman.[3]

The public derived no benefit from investment banks behaving like this. The Abacus transaction raised no financing for anyone and mired two European institutions in the structured credit market even more deeply than they already were. It had directly raised the risk and instability of the financial system.

But it was far from clear that Goldman had done anything illegal. The alleged offense was to permit Mr. Paulson to take part in selecting and screening which securities to include (although the final decision rested with a third party), and not mention this when selling the product to victim banks. Although unpleasant, it is hard to see how this behavior broke any law. A synthetic CDO requires someone to be "short." The "long" investors knew this. Whoever the "short" investor was, they plainly thought the subprime securities were a bad deal.

And, indeed, the law as it stood could do nothing to thwart such a damaging piece of business. The SEC settled out of court, with Goldman paying $550 million and admitting to making a "mistake" in its marketing documents but not acknowledging any wrongdoing. The fine was equivalent to only 1.2 percent of Goldman's 2009 revenues, although the lasting damage to its reputation may have been worth far more. Two years later, the Department of Justice announced that it would not be pressing charges. The behavior was amoral, if not reprehensible, but it was not illegal.

That outcome proved that the law itself was inadequate. The next critical task was to change the law to ensure that any future Abacus-style transactions were illegal. The sprawling Dodd-Frank Act, signed into law shortly after the Abacus charges were raised, failed to do this. Instead, it implemented the so-called Volcker Rule—named after the former Federal Reserve Chairman Paul Volcker who first proposed it—to force deposit-taking banks to divest their private equity and proprietary trading businesses. Dodd-Frank also forced the biggest, systemically important banks to take on extra capital to guard against fresh accidents. But it did not force banks to break up. And it did not ban products like Abacus.

In skirting the issue, the United States followed an international pattern. A special U.K. commission in 2011 said that banks should "ring-fence" their investment banking businesses, to keep money generated by the retail bank off-limits to them. That meant money from depositors could not be used to fund investment bets, but it stopped short of demanding a full company split. And internationally, a new Basel III agreement required banks to carry much more capital as a buffer against losses (which would reduce profits during good times) but gave them the best part of a decade to build up that capital. Across the Eurozone, huge financial conglomerates combining commercial banking with many riskier forms of finance were allowed to stay intact.

This was a different response than in the 1930s. Then, U.S. politicians were determined to ensure that no bad investment banking bets would ever bring down retail banks and their customers, and forced a complete split between investment and commercial banking, while making it hard for banks to grow. Such a tough approach was hard to adopt when governments had committed themselves to "muddle-through," aided by low interest rates, and when banks were arguing that the new measures would harm them just when the public needed a healthy banking system most.

Even this muted response sparked fierce opposition from Wall Street. The campaign against the Volcker Rule was led by Jamie Dimon, the charismatic CEO of JPMorgan. His institution combined both a sprawling investment bank and the Chase Manhattan retail banking empire, meaning that he was directly affected. Dimon complained bitterly that the Rule would make it harder for his bank to hedge against risks and to compete against foreign institutions. "Paul Volcker by his own admission has said he doesn't understand capital markets," he told Fox Business News. "He has proven that to me."[4]

As the efforts at re-regulation foundered, another problem appeared—the sheer amount of money that central banks had to create to deal with the issue. Even with interest rates effectively at zero, markets moved to every shift in monetary policy. As shown earlier, low U.S. rates distorted currencies across the world. Stock markets fell in the spring 2010 as Mr. Bernanke began to discuss "exit strategies" from extreme monetary policy—a euphemism for raising rates. U.S. stocks rallied that fall after he came through with QE2. In the U.K., with an even more damaged banking sector and a slower economy, the Bank of England then resorted to QE3—yet more purchases of bonds.

The Fed tried to be more imaginative in 2011. Faced with a sell-off of more than 20 percent in the stock market, as unemployment remained doggedly high, Mr. Bernanke announced Operation Twist. This involved taking the proceeds from short-term bonds that had expired and using them to buy longer-term bonds— effectively a way to push down longer-term interest rates. He also took the extraordinary step of promising not to raise rates until 2014, making it easy for banks to plan.

But the internal strains of the policy were ever more apparent. Bank lending remained sluggish, and signs of stress would reappear within weeks after each dose of stimulus was removed. Those banks that were not too big to fail tended to fail. In the seven years from 2000 to 2006, a total of only 24 banks failed in the United States. Then, 2009 saw 140 U.S. banks fail, the most since deposit insurance was introduced in the 1930s. That number rose to 157 in 2010, and another 91 failed in 2011.[5] Rising unemployment made it harder for people to pay their debts and brought higher defaults in its wake.

Courts grew restive about the leniency regulators were showing toward banks that appeared to have committed blatant fraud during the credit boom. Bitter battles ensued over foreclosures, as borrowers, often unemployed, struggled to stay in their houses. Politicians wanted the banks to go easy. But the banks, laden down with bad debts, could ill afford to do so. And if courts were restive, so were voters. Banks' big profits made them unpopular. In the summer of 2011, the Occupy Wall Street movement broke out across the United States, crystallizing understandable populist anger. It spread across the world, with a big tent city even forming around St Paul's Cathedral in the heart of London.

The bankers added to their own travails. In 2012, a Goldman Sachs banker, Greg Smith, resigned by way of a public letter in *The New York Times*, in which he alleged that Goldman bankers had lost their "moral fiber" and called their clients "muppets." "I attend derivatives sales meetings where not one single minute is spent asking questions about how we can help clients," he railed. "It's purely about how we can make the most possible money off of them."[6] It certainly seemed to fit the behavior that had created Abacus. Beyond the strong language, the point was the same as ever; bankers were not treating money as they would their own. Post-Lehman reforms, while creating great confusion and making it harder for them to make money, had not changed this.

Meanwhile, in May 2012, JPMorgan torpedoed Jamie Dimon's campaign against the Volcker Rule by announcing it had taken a one-time trading loss eventually estimated at about $5.8 billion, thanks to esoteric trades in credit derivatives. Adding to the embarrassment, it happened in a division of the bank that was supposed to deploy the bank's excess cash in such a way as to avoid taking excessive risks. Only months earlier, Dimon had derided press speculation about the huge position in certain credit derivatives that JPMorgan was taking in London, describing it as a tempest in a teacup. Dimon admitted that the bank had bungled badly and that "plays right into the hands of a bunch of pundits out there." He also said that the Volcker rule as then planned would not have prevented the trading—implying strongly that the rule had been watered down too much.[7]

Barclays bank of the U.K., owner of the former Lehman Brothers businesses in the U.S., caused a new scandal when it admitted that it had deliberately manipulated the interest rates used for setting many variable mortgage rates and other loans, which added to the furor. It had to pay a $450 million fine to regulators in various countries to settle the issue, while other banks remained under investigation.[8] Investment bankers had made themselves a better return by manipulating the rates on offer in the retail bank, adding to the arguments for a split.

No wonder, then, that the great rally in bank shares came to an end. After tripling in barely a year, the share prices of the biggest U.S. banks peaked in April 2010. After that they slid more than 44 percent. By late 2011, they were trading for about one-third less than their official book value, reflecting widespread belief that more big losses were in the pipeline. That called into question whether the markets could continue their virtuous circle until the banks had dealt with all the overhang of bad debt on their books. In the United States, this policy of muddling through stayed, just about, on track. Banks' loans were a smaller proportion of their deposits, a critical measure of their health and conservatism, than at any time in more than a decade.

The same, however, could not be said of Europe. Over this period, U.S. bank shares outperformed those of their Eurozone counterparts by some 69 percent. Many European banks came to trade for only a fraction of the official value on their books. Hampered by a central bank that was far more reluctant to print money, and by a banking system bigger and more unwieldy even than that of the United States, it was Europe that would put the attempt to "muddle through" to its critical test.

Summary

The United States, Europe, and multilateral authorities have failed to decide on credible new regulation for banks, whose reputation has progressively weakened thanks to a series of scandals.

- Aggressive selling by U.S. investment banks persuaded European banks to buy U.S. subprime debt before the crisis.

- Government re-regulation has stopped short of splitting up banks, but it has sharply crimped their profitability—arguably the worst of both worlds.

- In the United States, banks do appear steadily to be returning to health. The same is not true for Europe.

Endnotes

1. There is a lengthy discussion of complicated credit derivatives in *The Fearful Rise of Markets*.

2. See "Why bets on synthetic CDOs must be banned" by John Authers. *Financial Times*, April 23, 2010. http://www.ft.com/intl/cms/s/0/1302fcd6-4ef1-11df-b8f4-00144feab49a.html.

3. See *The Greatest Trade Ever: The Behind-The-Scenes Story of How John Paulson Defied Wall Street and Made Financial History* by Gregory Zuckerman. New York: Random House, 2009.

4. See http://www.foxbusiness.com/topics/markets/volcker-rule.htm?

5. Up-to-date statistics are available online at http://www.fdic.gov/bank/individual/failed/banklist.html.

6. See "Why I Am Leaving Goldman Sachs" by Greg Smith. *New York Times*, March 14, 2012. http://www.nytimes.com/2012/03/14/opinion/why-i-am-leaving-goldman-sachs.html?pagewanted=all.

7. See "Dimon is a Whale of a Hedge Fund Manager" by John Gapper. *Financial Times*, May 11, 2012.

8. See "Barclays fined a record £290m" by Brooke Masters, Caroline Binham, and Kara Scannell. *Financial Times*, June 27, 2012.

Chapter 7

Europe:
The Logic of Contagion

We have to be able to stop the financial markets.
We have the instruments of torture in the basement.
—Jean-Claude Juncker, prime minister of Luxembourg
and president of the Eurogroup, 2010

The Eurozone sovereign debt crisis erupted in spring 2010 and brought down a series of European governments which had desperately taken on their banks' debts in an attempt to deal with the financial crisis. It also revealed deep flaws in the structure of the Eurozone.

In May 2010, Athens erupted in riots. Greeks had reason for rage, as their politicians had let them down. Their government was indebted, and the new Prime Minister George Papandreou had recently admitted that its deficit was not between 6 and 8 percent of gross domestic product, as the outgoing government had claimed, but 12.5 percent.[1] This was a number that transformed perceptions of Greece and whether it could pay off its debts. Markets treated Greek debt the same way they had treated U.S. subprime debt a few years earlier; they sold it.

As a direct consequence, the interest rate on government debt rose, making it ever harder for the government to meet its debts. Mr. Papandreou tried to win investors around by admitting in a humiliating Brussels speech that Greece's "basic problem is systemic corruption."[2] But he had no choice but to ask the European Union for a "bailout" loan. Understandably, his creditors wanted proof that Greece could pay its debts in the future. So Mr. Papandreou slashed government services, which provoked fatal riots on the streets of Athens. Within a year, two other peripheral EU countries, Ireland and Portugal, also asked for bailouts; within two years Spain had been promised €100 billion to rescue its banks. The cost of debt for Italy, the third largest nation in the Eurozone, had also reached levels that implied it would need outside help. That forced the European Central Bank into a historic move that effectively printed more than 1 trillion euros. It also mired countries at the heart of Europe, such as France and the Netherlands, in damaging debates as politicians failed to agree on their own dose of austerity.

All this was predictable. The world's developed nations had survived the earlier credit crisis by putting their sovereign credit ratings behind their banks. As those banks were full of bad debts, those same government credit ratings now came into question. Judged as a whole, the Eurozone was in far better fiscal health than the United States or the United Kingdom, according to the International Monetary Fund's World Economic Outlook (see Figure 7.1). It had a fiscal deficit of approximately 4 percent of its gross domestic product entering 2011, less than half the U.S. deficit of approximately 10 percent. If every member of the zone stood behind all other countries' debts, there would be no crisis. But the Eurozone's flawed political construction meant that individual governments were weak, and markets tested every fissure.

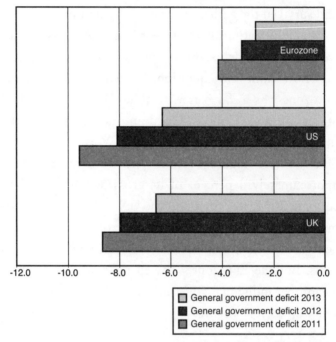

The Eurozone's Deficit Problem in Context

FIGURE 7.1   *Judged as a whole, the Eurozone did not have a fiscal problem. Its total deficit was much smaller, as a proportion of the economy, than the deficits of either the United States or the United Kingdom.*

Not all the afflicted countries suffered the same problems. Greece's maladies were a chronically inefficient public sector and endemic tax evasion. Meanwhile, Ireland suffered primarily from its 2008 decision, made days after Lehman, to guarantee all its bank deposits. Those banks were in trouble in the first place because Ireland, like the United States, had enjoyed its own property bubble, driven by the country's deliberate expansion as an offshore financial center. Just before the crisis, Ireland's government debt was only 25 percent of GDP; three years later, the debts on banks' books had raised this to 98 percent. Unlike Greece, Ireland had a healthy and booming economy entering the crisis; its problem was that it had financed it, through its banks, in a way that proved far too risky.

Portugal effectively wasted its euro membership, growing at only 1.1 percent per year from 2001 to 2007, whereas its Spanish neighbor was booming.[3] And Spain suffered the after-effects of its own domestic property boom, abetted by an inefficient system of housing banks known as *cajas*. These were similar to U.S. savings and loans and were often used as the fiefs for local politicians. Collectively, they poured money into the coffers of property developers who used them to embark on poorly thought-out construction projects for which there was little demand—and kept themselves popular with their local governments by pouring the profits, while they existed, into big social projects such as museums and parks.

After this bubble burst, Spain's federal structure made it particularly hard to implement Greek-style austerity. Spain is divided into large regions with their own strong sense of identity, and in several cases their own language, such as Catalonia, Andalusia, and the Basque

Country. Each region controlled its own basic services and tended to believe that it had suffered the steepest cuts. Spanish unemployment surged to more than 20 percent by 2010, making it still harder to cut government spending.

As for Italy, it had avoided a property bubble and did not have a big deficit. Its problem was its huge government bond market, which is the largest in Europe—even bigger than the market for German bunds—meaning that the debt costs a lot to service. That made Italy especially vulnerable to any rise in interest rates. Furthermore, its political credibility descended into farce under its playboy Prime Minister Silvio Berlusconi, the dominant figure in Italian politics since 1994. As scandals multiplied, with prosecutors alleging that the septuagenarian premier had slept with 33 women in the space of two months,[4] Mr. Berlusconi's image became hopelessly tarnished just as Italy needed a credible leader to hold the markets at bay.

As in the southeast Asian crisis a decade earlier, high indebtedness and the after-effects of property bubbles co-existed with artificially strong currencies. The critical difference: Asian nations had retained their own currencies and merely pegged them to the dollar. Their crisis could be resolved by devaluation. Greece and the others did not have that option because they no longer had their own currency.

In a way, the countries of southern Europe had inflicted second-class status on themselves by surrendering the ability to borrow in their own currency. Certainly, markets perceived euro membership as a terrible handicap. Spain lurched into crisis despite having outstanding government debt of only approximately 40 percent of its GDP. Meanwhile, the U.K. had debt of 94 percent of its GDP and entered a double-dip recession, but it retained its own currency and avoided a crisis.[5]

Leaving the euro might appear the natural response, even given the great practical difficulties. But Europe badly wanted to avoid setting the precedent that a country could exit, as this would embolden speculators to attack other countries. Moreover, if Greece were to leave the euro, its currency would lose much of its value, bringing down the value of any Greek investments. Banks that had lent to Greek companies faced serious losses. And once such a precedent had been set, banks and investors would naturally try to avert the risk of this happening elsewhere by pulling their money out of other countries that might leave the euro. Finally, most Greeks did not want the humiliation, or economic pain, of exiting the euro.

With devaluation not an option, markets expressed their loss of confidence in Greece by selling its debt, meaning that it needed to pay a higher rate of interest on its loans. This is what trapped Greece. In 2010, its outstanding debt was only equivalent to 34 percent of its GDP, and the government's primary deficit, excluding the cost of paying its debt, was approximately 5 percent of the GDP. This was below the deficits in the U.K., Japan, or the United States. When interest payments were included, however, Greece's deficit rose to 10.4 percent of the GDP—higher than that of any of the world's biggest economies, and far more than it could be trusted to repay.

This presented a problem for all the Eurozone. But Europe lacked the political institutions to respond quickly. Even the U.S. Congress seemed efficient compared to a body coordinating policy across 17 countries.

Furthermore, Europe's politicians were undercut by the weakness of their banks. Indeed, the European sovereign and banking crises were almost indistinguishable. Europe was burdened with banking systems that could not be allowed to fail, but which governments did not have the power to rescue. The banks also held Eurozone government bonds as their chief "risk-free" assets. A downgrade of the bonds by the rating agencies (which would require banks to put aside more capital to protect against losses) or partial defaults that would cause the bonds' value to be partially written down (known as "haircuts"), could easily render Europe's banking system insolvent. Fixing that would require more public money, thus worsening the governments' credit and creating a vicious circle.

So, at all costs, Europe's leaders wanted to avoid a bailout at taxpayer expense, a default that might trigger a banking collapse or an exit from the euro that also risked a banking collapse, while endangering a much-cherished political project.

Thus, their response was to load the burden onto Greece. The rest of the Eurozone nations, and the International Monetary Fund (IMF), were prepared to lend the country €110 billion—but only in return for austerity cuts that would slash Greek living standards.[6] To back this up, they also tried to impress the markets with a show of strength. Politicians thrashed out a European Financial Stability Facility (EFSF), which would backstop any country that got into trouble. With the core European nations' impeccable credit ratings behind it, it had the capacity to lend up to €440 billion, with the possibility to bring in extra funds from the IMF.[7]

The idea was that the EFSF's mere existence would intimidate any speculators who were considering betting on a euro break-up. It would wind down in 2013, without ever making a loan. Meanwhile, Greece's tough austerity measures would steadily solve its deficit problem. It did not happen that way.

In November 2010, Ireland took a bailout of €85 billion from the EU and from the International Monetary Fund. This went mostly to recapitalize its banks, which had by now forced the government to pay up assistance equivalent to one-half of Ireland's entire gross domestic product.[8]

Only six months later, Portugal had to follow with its own rescue of €78 billion.[9] Over the next three years, it agreed to cut its deficit to 3 percent of GDP, despite forecasts that its economy would continue to contract. It also agreed to freeze public sector pay and pensions for two years. Without violence, Portugal went through its own political convulsion. When Prime Minister José Socrates attempted to pass his fourth austerity program in a year, parliament voted it down, forcing a June 2011 election, which he lost.

In each case, governments threw in the towel as the prices of their outstanding bonds sagged. They asked for aid when the yield on their debt had risen above 7 percent—a level at which traders believed they could not finance themselves without extra help. This rule of thumb made speculative attacks that much easier. Traders referred to the crisis nations by the acronym PIIGS (Portugal, Italy, Ireland, Greece, Spain) and behaved as though the problems of these very different countries were identical (see Figure 7.2). The EU did the same, demanding much the same austerity from Greece, Ireland, and Portugal, even though the causes of their problems were different (see Figure 7.3).

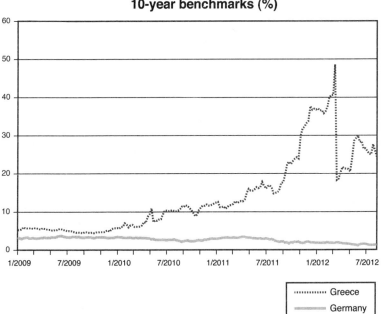

Government Bond Yields
10-year benchmarks (%)

FIGURE 7.2   *After investors lost confidence in Greek debt, they sold its bonds, and Greek borrowing costs soared. Meanwhile, they parked their funds in the safety of Germany, whose borrowing costs fell.*

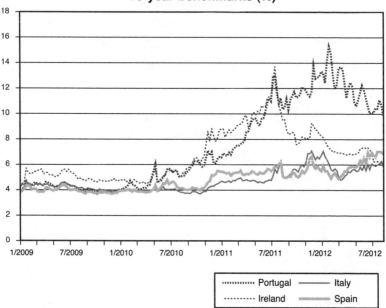

Government Bond Yields
10-year benchmarks (%)

Portugal ··········
Ireland ·········
Italy ———
Spain ▬▬▬

FIGURE 7.3 *Contagion had a logic. Traders saw that once a country's bond yield exceeded 7 percent, it tended to need to ask for an external bailout; and so pressure moved from one country to another.*

None of the measures the EU had taken to quell the crisis did much good. Instead, investors worked out that the EFSF—particularly after it had paid out to Portugal and Ireland—did not have the money to rescue Spain or Italy. Europe had not erected the strong firewall it needed. It was not even clear that more money for the

EFSF would help. All this would do was put extra pressure on the countries at the Eurozone's core, as they would have to take on their weaker brethren's debts.

Late in 2011, yields on Spanish and Italian debt moved above 6 percent, amid an air of panic. Now, investors began to sell the debt of France. The Eurozone's second biggest economy, and a triple-A credit, France's government budget came to 53.7 percent of GDP, more than any other Eurozone member, while its exports were lagging.[10] So the logic was inexorable; the more money France would have to put forward to rescue other countries in Europe, the more pressure that would put on its own finances. The extra spread payable for French bonds compared to German bunds rose above a full percentage point for the first time since the common currency was adopted. The market's message was that it did not believe the "core" countries had enough money to bail out both Spain and Italy without running into fiscal trouble themselves.

Meanwhile, as 2011 continued, an awful truth about Greece grew ever clearer. It had implemented the austerity cuts as agreed, but they were not helping. Cutting jobs and benefits in the public sector also cut life out of the economy. Unemployment, running at 11.7 percent when the first bailout was announced in the spring of 2010, virtually doubled to 22.6 percent over the next two years. Such an appalling recession inevitably meant that tax receipts fell. It was further than ever from financing itself.

Capital flowed out of the country. Far from solving the problem, the first bailout had given foreign investors and rich Greeks the valuable chance to take their money out of the country—an issue that would threaten other bailed-out countries after they had received their assistance.[11] By the beginning of 2012, the money held on deposit in Greek banks had dropped by one-third compared to the beginning of 2010 before the bailout. Europe's first strategy to deal with the crisis, of forcing austerity on the Greeks while trying to intimidate the markets with the money in the stability facility, had decisively failed. Now, Greece needed new relief and quickly.

Summary

When Greece revealed in late 2009 that it could not finance its deficit, the initial European response was to bail out the country in return for promised austerity cuts, while trying to persuade markets that no other countries would ever need a bailout. It failed.

- Euro-exit was dangerous because the Greek currency would devalue, and so the value of all Greek assets held by foreign banks would immediately fall.

- Any exit would set a dangerous precedent; it would show that other nations might also exit, and encourage investors to pull capital from them.

- Bailouts put pressure on the finances of the Eurozone's core nations.

- Market moves were self-fulfilling; when confidence in a country's debt was lost, the cost of servicing that debt soon grew prohibitive, making default or bailout more likely.

- Austerity—reducing government spending—failed to solve the problem because it also reduced growth, and so weakened governments' tax income.

Endnotes

1. See "Greece vows action to cut budget deficit" by Tony Barber. *Financial Times*, October 20, 2009.

2. See "Greece admits it is riddled with corruption" by Tony Barber. *Financial Times*, December 11, 2009 http://www.ft.com/intl/cms/s/0/54f4983e-e637-11de-bcbe-00144feab49a.html.

3. See "Portugal: too much carrot, not enough stick," in The Lex Column. *Financial Times*, May 4, 2011: http://www.ft.com/intl/cms/s/3/85e4c092-766c-11e0-b05b-00144feabdc0.html.

4. See, for example, "Silvio Berlusconi: sex with 33 women in two months? I'm 75!" *The Guardian*, March 16, 2011.

5. See, for example, "An Impeccable Disaster" by Paul Krugman, *The New York Times*, September 12, 2011.

6. See "Eurozone agrees €110bn Greece loans" by Kerin Hope, Nikki Tait, and Quentin Peel. *Financial Times*, May 2, 2010.

7. See "Europe pins hopes on special fund" by David Oakley. *Financial Times*, June 10, 2010.

8. See "Ireland" note, The Lex Column. *Financial Times*, November 29, 2010: http://www.ft.com/intl/cms/s/3/f7d2da66-fb9e-11df-b79a-00144feab49a.html.

9. See "Portugal reaches deal on 78bn bail-out" by Peter Wise in Lisbon. *Financial Times*, May 3, 2011.

10. See *The 2011 Euro Plus Monitor: Progress Amid the Turmoil*, by Holger Schmieding (principal author), published by Berenberg Bank and the Lisbon Council.

11. See "Spanish contagion," ft.com interview with Michael Gallagher of IDEAGlobal, June 13, 2012: http://video.ft.com/v/1686665047001/Spanish-contagion.

Chapter 8

Democrats Versus Technocrats

If we do not change our path, austerity threatens to force us out of the euro with even greater certainty.
—Alexis Tsipras, leader of Greek left-wing party SYRIZA, 2012

Europe's problem ultimately proved to be political. Either the periphery had to suffer austerity (over the passionate opposition of their voters), or voters in the core had to be persuaded to bail them out.

In June 2012, more than two years after riots greeted Greece's first big bailout, the world's attention was again fixed on the streets of Athens. Greece was holding a general election. Membership of the euro was at stake. Passions boiled over. In one televised debate, the leader of Golden Dawn, a neo-fascist party, literally came to blows with a communist leader, rising from his chair to strike her.[1] Tellingly, both extremes of the political spectrum had a chance to collect votes. Markets, meanwhile, braced themselves for a repeat of the "Lehman moment" four years earlier.

Why the angst? A May 2012 election ended in deadlock. Three successive parties had been offered the chance to form a government and failed. Votes collapsed for PASOK and New Democracy, the center-left and center-right parties who had alternated in power for decades. But if Greeks rejected the old order, they had no clear new savior. Instead, they flirted with both the extreme right and the extreme left.

Greeks had reached the point of simple refusal to accept the economic medicine that Europe was prescribing. As far as the voters were concerned, the deal that PASOK had signed with the rest of Europe to secure a second financial bail-out was unforgivable. It not only weakened the economy but tore up the social compact. For example, a Cretan 55-year-old shop-owner had paid regularly in to her pension fund and had expected a pension of €900 a month from the age of 60. Under the new deal, she had to continue paying until she was 67, when she would start receiving a monthly pension of €430—far short of a viable income.[2]

In short, the efforts of technocrats to appease market demands had collided head-on with democracy. And the same problem beset the rest of Europe in only slightly less virulent forms. As government after government responsible for the crisis went down to defeat, the short-term solution was to suspend democracy. But that could not work for long. Ultimately, it was not clear how any democratically elected politician could ever agree to inflict such pain on their voters. Greece, once the historic pioneer of democracy, unhappily became the exemplar of this problem for the rest of the continent.

At first, it appeared to be a technical problem. When the Greek government of George Papandreou decided to pursue a second bailout, private sector banks—and not the Greek voters—seemed to be the toughest negotiators. The latter half of 2011 saw interminable negotiations over "private sector involvement"—a euphemism for how big a loss banks would take on their Greek government bonds. There were also desperate measures to avoid saying Greece was in "default," because that would trigger payouts on credit default swaps—meaning losses for banks that had insured Greek bonds. Nervous about the effect this would have, negotiators thrashed out justifications for denying that a default had occurred, even if they had just agreed that Greece would not repay its debts in full.

The negotiations came to nothing. In the event, the banks wrote down their Greek government bonds by 53 percent, and insurers were required to pay out for a "default." And in return for appalling austerity,

Mr. Papandreou received a promise of an extra €130 billion in assistance.[3]

At the same time, finance ministers tried to arm themselves with a "big bazooka"—a financial response so vast that it would make futile any speculative attempt to force the Eurozone apart. In effect they repeated the 2010 measures that had failed, only with even more money and even more austerity. Some wanted a forced bank recapitalization so that any haircut for Greek bonds would not bankrupt the banks. This, after all, was how Hank Paulson had staunched the U.S. banking crisis in late 2008.

But any such bazooka had to be armed with money from taxpayers in Europe's core. Technocrats' plans had already collided with the wishes of voters in the periphery. In February 2011, the government of Prime Minister Brian Cowen was swept from power in the worst defeat for an incumbent government since Ireland had adopted its constitution in 1921. Portugal's government followed four months later.

Then in November 2011, the crisis felled elected prime ministers in Spain, Italy, and Greece. José Luis Rodriguez Zapatero, Spain's premier since 2004, received less than 30 percent of the vote, his party's worst showing in four decades. Mariano Rajoy, a center-right politician, succeeded him.

At this point, the greatest concern was Italy, whose borrowing costs now exceeded Spain's, while the scandals surrounding Mr. Berlusconi's colorful nightlife multiplied. Markets brought him down. Within one week of Italian government bond yields exceeding the dreaded 7 percent mark, he lost his majority in parliament and resigned as part of a deal in which parliament passed sweeping austerity measures. The premiership passed to Mario Monti, a professional economist and former European Union commissioner. For all the stains on Mr. Berlusconi's reputation, this was a direct victory for markets over an elected politician—an ugly precedent for anyone who believes in democracy.

A different fate was in store for Mr. Papandreou in Greece. His mandate still had years to run, but in the same month, November 2011, he declared that the terms of Greece's bailout should be put to a referendum. Because he had never suggested such a contingency during the protracted bailout negotiations, Europe's other politicians were outraged. Markets suffered what became known as the "Papandreou plunge." Greek borrowing costs shot up, Mr. Papandreou lost the support of his cabinet and resigned, ending what had been a distinguished political career. He was replaced, like Mr. Berlusconi, by a technocrat. Lucas Papademos, the new premier, was a former deputy governor of the European Central Bank. His task was to implement the austerity cuts that Greece had agreed upon, and then hand the country over to its moment of truth at the polls in the summer of 2012.

These political earthquakes left Germany and France in a quandary. If austerity did not work, and money-printing was unacceptable, only three options remained: changing the Eurozone, shrinking it, or abandoning it. The Eurozone could not survive as it was, because markets could keep picking off its members at will. So it must either get smaller, jettisoning its weaker members, or change its rules so that each country's treasury plainly stood behind all the others—a move that implied a common fiscal policy, maybe even a common treasury, and a loss of sovereignty. Ideally, as far as markets were concerned, there would be "euro-bonds"—issued and repayable by all Eurozone nations jointly. With German finances by far the strongest in the continent, it also implied that Germans would pay off the debts of other countries. German voters understandably objected to this.

Furthermore, whatever changes were wrought in the Eurozone, it had to do something to shore up its banks. Modern banking made it very easy for customers to move their deposits from one country to another. This could undermine ingenious plans to keep the zone together. Universal deposit insurance—to remove all incentives to move funds out of a country—was necessary. But that implied some form of common regulation to oversee all of the banks—which implied more political problems, as countries might have to give up the chance to regulate their own banks.

The outlines of a compromise existed. A deal was reached in the small hours of the Brussels morning of December 9, 2011, after a series of emergency summits. Angela Merkel, Germany's chancellor, and France's President Nicolas Sarkozy, agreed that all nations needed tighter fiscal integration, and that countries would face penalties for exceeding their target deficits. They hoped this would prompt the ECB to help out with fresh funds. But the U.K. refused to go along, with its Prime Minister David Cameron casting its vote against. With the banking centre of the City of London so central to his country's competitiveness, he argued that he had no alternative. This diplomatic saga served only to undermine market confidence.

The dynamic was now identical to the Lehman Brothers crisis in the United States some three years earlier. Elected politicians could not raise the money from tax-payers, so it would have to be created by the central bank. Politicians wanted the European Central Bank (ECB) to buy as many Italian bonds as it took to keep the nation's borrowing costs manageable. This was the easiest political way out, as the ECB had the power to print money—even if this risked inflation later on. But until this point, the ECB had refused to create money in the same way that the Federal Reserve had done in the

United States; as a percentage of gross domestic product, the Fed had bought five times more bonds than the ECB.

Mario Draghi, the Italian who took over the bank in autumn 2011, was a smart politician. He found a way around the problem. The ECB could not lend to governments, but it could lend to banks. And those banks could, in turn, lend to governments by buying their bonds. In December 2011, and again in February 2012, the ECB offered to lend European banks funds that they could keep for three years at an interest rate of only 1 percent. The banks had to put up collateral to get the loans, but crucially this collateral could be troubled debt from countries like Spain or Italy. The banks now had no need to sell those bonds for three years and could also refinance loans that they would otherwise have had to repay. This financial engineering averted an imminent "credit crunch"; the ECB's own surveys showed that recipient banks were preparing to tighten the standards they applied to any new loans.

But it had other effects. Banks could make a *carry trade*: Buy the bonds yielding more than 5 percent, borrow at 1 percent, and feast on the difference for three years. So they bought (largely from international investors happy to escape), and yields came down—which in itself eased governments' problems. Within weeks, Italian bond yields were below 5 percent, and the nation was out of crisis for a while.

The maneuver had a cynical logic, explained by the hedge fund manager George Soros. There was no reason for a bank not to load up on its own government's debt. If that debt ever defaulted, the bank would be out of business anyway. The ECB's move was intended to convince investors that there would be no bank collapse that could force a sovereign default—or in other words, that the banking and sovereign crises were not inextricably linked. And yet ironically, it led the biggest Spanish and Italian banks to load up on even more Spanish and Italian government debt, tying the fates of banks and their governments even more closely together. According to the ECB, the proportion of Spain's debt held by its banks rose from below 10 percent to almost 30 percent within weeks of receiving the funding.

But even this only engineered a brief respite. The problem remained the same. More measures were needed to deal with outstanding debts, and those measures could not be reconciled with democracy. In the spring of 2012, the Eurozone lurched back into crisis.

As Spain was afflicted by general strikes and violence, the new premier Mariano Rajoy announced unilaterally that he was shifting his deficit target for the year to 5.8 percent of GDP, from 4.4 percent of GDP. Even this more lenient target required a 17 percent cut in government spending and a 6 percent rise in electricity prices, but his backtracking slowed the timetable for Spain to return to surplus and annoyed traders. Borrowing costs began to rise once more.

In May, the French elected Francois Hollande, a Socialist who favored "growth" over "austerity," as their new president, while the Greeks elected a new parliament dominated by fringe parties who rejected the terms of the country's bailout. The implications were profound; if Greeks refused to go through with austerity cuts, they would be calling the bluff of the rest of the EU. If the EU did not blink, and refused to pay as promised, Greece would inevitably default by the end of 2012. Could it possibly stay in the euro in those circumstances? With all this in the balance, a new election was scheduled for June 17.

On May 25, Bankia, the biggest of Spain's troublesome housing banks or *cajas*, at last admitted that it needed €19 billion in new capital. Many of its loans were to property developers and backed by real estate whose value was now clearly lower but difficult to estimate. Few properties were changing hands, making it hard to value them. Spain's government had to find the money for Bankia somewhere, so Mr. Rajoy swallowed his pride and requested a bailout package for his country's banks of €100 billion. The bailout was announced a week before Greece went to the polls.[4]

In the weeks that followed, Spain's regions started to demand help from Madrid, and everyone looked toward the big repayments the country had to make in the fall of 2012. Bond yields were above 7 percent. If the markets were to be believed, a bailout for Spain itself, and not just its banks, was inevitable.

And yet the electorates of the countries that could afford to bail it out were evidently not prepared to do so. And even if they did, everything now pointed to the need for what financiers called "debt mutualization"— getting all of the Eurozone countries to stand behind the debt of each member. Truly mutualized debt, as in euro-bonds, would solve the problem in an instant. But mutualization also implied that the taxpayers of countries like Germany and Finland, with impeccable finances, would finance profligate countries.

This was not a mere question of nationalism. Germany had benefited from low interest rates in the earlier part of the decade, and the perverse dynamics of the Eurozone had enabled it to sell more of its exports to fast-growing countries like Spain. But Germany had also undergone a painful improvement in productivity, meaning that its workers had gone without wage increases in return for working harder. According to the Organization for Economic Cooperation and Development, Germans produced $55.30 in gross domestic product for each hour they worked (while other core countries produced even more); in Greece and Portugal the figures were $33.90 and $32.50 (although productivity in Spain was much more respectable at $48.10).[5] Now the fruits of those labors were to go to other countries who had not endured that pain. That was a political sticking point.

Angela Merkel, Germany's chancellor, was in an impossible position, and announced that her attitude to debt mutualization was "over my dead body." In June 2012 she went so far as to say "I don't see total debt liability as long as I live."[6] But traders calculated that she faced much the same dilemma the American government had suffered before Lehman. The administration of George W. Bush had concluded that it was politically untenable to bail out greedy bankers two months before an election. But Mrs. Merkel, who faced an election in 2013, now knew that the principled alternative they had chosen had led to economic collapse and electoral defeat. The steady decline into recession across the Eurozone made life even more difficult.

At some point, it seemed that voters somewhere, either in the core or the periphery, must decisively end the technocrats' attempts to play for time and reconcile the Eurozone's profound differences. That, in turn, could easily be Europe's "Lehman moment."

Markets braced for just such a moment if Greeks voted to reject the country's bailout in their June election.[7] It did not happen. New Democracy, the old center-right grouping, and PASOK had enough parliamentary seats between them to form a government. But SYRIZA, the far left anti-bailout party, gained 27.5 percent of the vote. In total, more than 57 percent of votes had gone to parties that wanted to reject Europe's terms; the victory for the old-line parties owed more to the vagaries of the Greek electoral system than it did to any popular support for austerity.[8] On such a thin margin, Europe avoided its Lehman moment and stock markets enjoyed a new rally, which was soon buoyed by promises from the ECB that it would do "whatever it takes" to keep the euro intact, followed later by the announcement of Outright Monetary Transactions (OMTs) to buy the bonds of countries that requested a bailout. But the risk remains that that moment was not averted, but merely delayed.

Summary

Europe's problem is essentially political. It collectively has the money to pay its debts, but it is not clear that democratic politicians can convince their electorates to endorse the reforms to pool debt that markets demand.

- Economic damage is inevitable.

- Measures to pool payments of debt include:

    - Allowing the European Central Bank, which can print money, to buy peripheral nations' bonds on the open market without limit

    - Allowing the European Stability Mechanism, using taxpayers' money, to buy peripheral bonds directly

    - A new "banking union" where all Eurozone banks would receive generous deposit insurance (funded by Eurozone taxpayers)

    - "Euro-bonds"—bonds issued by the Eurozone as a whole rather than by countries—meaning that taxpayers in each country would stand behind the taxpayers of all the others.

- Voters across the Eurozone had political objections to all these plans.

Endnotes

1. This astonishing incident has been well viewed on YouTube: http://www.youtube.com/watch?v=Xi6Tb LmeFoQ.

2. These details cover a person interviewed by the author.

3. See "Greece launches debt swap offer" by David Oakley, Mary Watkins and Kerin Hope. *Financial Times*, February 24, 2012: http://www.ft. com/intl/cms/s/0/cd8953dc-5ee1-11e1-a087-00144feabdc0.html.

4. See "Rajoy presents Spain bailout as victory" by Victor Mallet and Peter Spiegel. *Financial Times*, June 11, 2012. http://www.ft.com/intl/cms/s/0/ 4599be98-b2ed-11e1-83a9-00144feabdc0.html.

5. See http://stats.oecd.org/Index.aspx?DatasetCode= LEVEL.

6. See "Merkel: no EU total debt liability in my life" by Reuters: http://www.reuters.com/article/2012/ 06/26/us-eurozone-merkel-debt-idUSBRE85 P0YR20120626.

7. For a broad discussion of these issues, see *If Greece goes?: The impact of a Greek default on Europe and the world economy*, e-book published by the *Financial Times*: http://www.amazon.co.uk/If-Greece-goes-default-ebook/dp/B008846SEW/ ref=sr_1_1?s=books&ie=UTF8&qid=1344872011 &sr=1-1.

8. Full results are available at: http://ekloges.ypes.gr/ v2012b/public/index.html?lang=en#{"cls":"main", "params":{}}.

Chapter 9

Risk-On, Risk-Off Markets

*Without due recognition of crowd-thinking (which
often seems crowd-madness) our theories of economics
leave much to be desired. It is a force wholly
impalpable—perhaps little amenable to analysis and
less to guidance—and yet, knowledge of it is necessary
to right judgments on passing events.*
—Bernard Baruch, American financier, stock-market
speculator, statesman, and political consultant, writing
in 1934

The 2009 rally in U.S. stocks was the most impressive in a century, and not even the Eurozone crisis could throw it into reverse. But this was achieved amid record prices for gold and treasury bonds, leaving many to fear it had been achieved only through government intervention and monetary debasement.

The Eurozone crisis interrupted possibly the greatest global stock market rally in more than a century. At its

March 2009 nadir, the S&P 500 hit the ominous level of 666, no higher than it had been in August 1996. From there, it regained in 8 months exactly one-half its losses of the previous 16 months, and by May 2011, barely 2 years later, it had doubled.

What is remarkable is that the crisis in the Eurozone merely interrupted that rally; it did not send it into reverse. By the summer of 2012, when the crisis had already forced bailouts for four European countries, U.S. stocks were still twice their value of 2009. The S&P's recovery was far ahead of the "relief rallies" following history's other great crashes.

Four years after its October 2007 all-time high, the S&P was down by only 25 percent. By comparison, four years after the 1929 Great Crash, and after the 1990 collapse of the Japanese stock market, the Dow Industrials and Nikkei 225 were still down 73 and 55 percent, respectively (see Figure 9.1).

There were some reasons to buy stocks during this period, such as a China-led global economic recovery (even though the world economy was showing signs of rolling over into a new recession by 2012). Also, companies' profits were strong because they had used the post-Lehman downturn to cut costs by firing workers. That meant record margins when business returned. But the nature of the business cycle dictates that these margins are likely to fall. And these factors alone could not explain such a strong rally in the face of overwhelming evidence from Europe that the global financial system remained stricken.

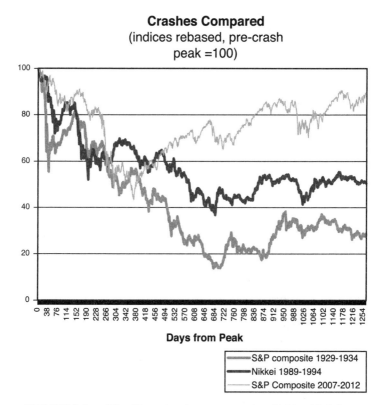

Crashes Compared
(indices rebased, pre-crash peak =100)

Days from Peak

S&P composite 1929-1934
Nikkei 1989-1994
S&P Composite 2007-2012

FIGURE 9.1   *After history's other great crashes, in New York in 1929 and in Japan after 1989, stock markets took a long time to recover. Why has the U.S. stock market recovered so quickly this time?*

Far from showing confidence in Uncle Sam, the U.S. market's fearful rise in the teeth of the crisis in Europe rested on the same pathologies that had over the previous decade created the bubbles in tech stocks, and then in house prices and sub-prime credit. Once viewed through the lens of the markets that set the price of money—foreign exchange, commodities and bonds—stocks' recovery looked hollow.

Investors put their panic behind them only after extraordinary interventions by the U.S. and Chinese governments that must, at some point, be paid for. In the long run, that could be a drag on share prices and on the economy. But in the short run, by making the price of money cheaper, these actions directly forced the stock market upward.

In March 2009, the first dose of quantitative easing (QE1) by the Fed jolted markets back to life, as it expanded the money supply by buying back Treasury bonds. This pushed down their yields (see Figure 9.2). The following summer, after QE1 had been completed, Ben Bernanke started discussing ways to withdraw the stimulus—and short-term interest rates rose in response, while stocks fell and confidence sagged. Then in late August at a speech in Jackson Hole, Wyoming, he signaled that QE2—another dose of bond purchases—was on its way and ignited another rally. The pattern repeated with Operation Twist and QE3 in 2012. Such desperation for central banks to keep priming the pump with loose money demonstrated an utter lack of confidence in the economy. Investors knew Mr.

Bernanke would never have resorted to such measures unless the economy was in deep trouble. But because the Fed was holding the returns available from bank deposits and bonds at historically low levels, they had little choice but to buy stocks. The government was virtually daring them to take a risk.

The S&P since the Peak with Fed Policy Actions

FIGURE 9.2 *The pattern is clear. Whenever the Federal Reserve announced that it was intervening with cheaper money, markets recovered. QE3 followed in September 2012.*

This cheap money calls stocks' true value into question. In dollar terms, the S&P doubled from its low in March 2009. But in terms of "harder" currencies, to which investors moved funds in response to falling U.S. interest rates, the rally in American stocks was far less impressive. Valued in terms of gold, the S&P barely ever rose above its March 2009 low. Five years later, it was less than one-half its 2007 high. Arguably, gold is in a bubble; but valued in Japanese yen, the S&P was still down by more than one-third from its high. The point is unavoidable: When measured in hard currency, the S&P has barely recovered (see Figure 9.3).

The S&P Since the Peak in Terms of Gold and the Yen

FIGURE 9.3   *Valued in dollars, the S&P 500 appears to have recovered well. Valued in harder currencies, like gold or the Japanese yen, it has not.*

On this basis, rather than rallying, investors were merely yielding to government pressure when they bought stocks. The remarkable phenomenon in the years after Lehman was not the doubling of the stock market, but rather the stunning performance of the Treasury bond market.

To put this in perspective, remember that U.S. banks' recovery relied on co-opting, or abusing, the U.S. government's credit rating. From 2009 onward, the United States stood as the ultimate guarantor of U.S. banks' debt. It could issue more debt because its credit was rated higher than any other nation's. As we have seen, this strategy worked, but it was a dangerous one with uncomfortable parallels. In the Eurozone, governments' sovereign credit ratings were downgraded after they took on the extra expense of bailing out banks. But this owed much to the unique strains imposed on the Eurozone's crisis-hit countries by the single currency. A more relevant—and even more uncomfortable— analogy might be with American International Group (AIG), before the crash in 2008. AIG's AAA rating, although undeserved, enabled many securities to trade for more than they were worth. Its downgrade was a moment of truth for the market. That credit rating, it was soon revealed, had been virtually the only thing keeping many of Europe's banks solvent. That is why the United States had to step in to guarantee AIG's debts.

Much the same would happen—although of course this time with no guarantor of last resort to step in—if the market were ever to lose its confidence in the United States. As bond yields have fallen steadily since 1982, most bond traders now working have no experience in dealing with a "bear market" turn in bonds. This means that any such loss of confidence could easily lead to panic and much higher rates. Indeed, when Standard & Poor's cut the U.S. credit rating from AAA in summer 2011, after the new Republican majority in the House of Representatives had threatened to force a default, markets suffered a swoon.

But they recovered within months, and bond yields went on to set new record lows. In the summer of 2012, yields on treasury debt (and on the debt of strong European countries that appeared to be at much greater risk from the Eurozone crisis, such as Germany, France, and the United Kingdom) were at historic lows, making the debt expensive to hold. That can only make sense if investors are confident that no default is on the horizon.

Given all the reasons for concern, how can investors possibly be so confident? The logic remained intact; the U.S. government has tax-raising powers, and the Fed can print as much of the world's reserve currency as it likes. A U.S. default, despite everything, should therefore be a long way off.

That leads to a perverse way in which the U.S. has benefited from the crisis in the Eurozone. Debts underwritten by large countries with the power to print their own currency remain as much of a "safe haven" as anything in the midst of the Eurozone crisis. As money exited the periphery of the Eurozone, it had to go somewhere—and the destination was usually either U.S. Treasuries or German bunds. Once 10-year bunds and Treasuries promise to yield barely one percent over 10 years, far less than stocks would likely produce in dividends, then the case for investors to buy some stocks grows ever stronger. So the flow of money out of Europe makes American debt more expensive (while making it ever cheaper for Uncle Sam to borrow), and therefore encourages U.S. investors to buy stocks instead. Comparing the yields on bonds with the dividend yields paid by stocks, stocks have never seemed such good value (see Figure 9.4).

U.S. Equity and Bond Yields (%)

Dividend Yield on S&P Composite
Government 10-year bond yield

FIGURE 9.4   *U.S. stocks have not offered such good value relative to bonds in more than half a century. Is that because stocks are too cheap, or because bonds are too expensive?*

However, pressure to buy bonds is not all good news for stocks. Indeed, in the longer term it could act as a brake. Governments have the power to force people to buy their bonds. Such a policy is known as *financial repression*—a term popularized by the academic Carmen Reinhart[1]—and governments have every incentive to resort to it when they have taken on huge debts to quell a crisis. Huge bulk-buying of bonds by central banks is only one form of repression. New rules for pension funds and insurers have required them to hold far more bonds, and far fewer stocks, as they try to show that they can guarantee the payouts they have promised to pensioners. In aggregate, these regulations drove massive changes. In the United States and the United Kingdom, public pension funds had allocations to equities as high as 70 percent as recently as 2002. They are now down to 40 percent in the U.K. and 52 percent in the U.S.[2] Big investment institutions complain that as bonds get dearer and stocks cheaper, their regulators force them against all orthodoxy of financial prudence, to buy bonds.[3] If the U.S. bond market does finally blow up, as much feared, pension funds—not for the first time—will suffer more than most.

There is every reason to expect financial repression to carry on for a while. It is politically expedient. Therefore, bond prices could stay fixed at a high level for a while. In the long term, this will drag on stocks, as many investors will be forced to buy something else. But low bond prices will also continue to make the dividends paid out by stocks look appealing. In other words, this is an argument for markets to move sideways. Stocks do indeed look historically cheap relative to bonds. The fact that stocks have not rallied far more shows underlying lack of confidence in stocks.

Historic valuations provide further evidence that the 2009 rally was driven more by the government's intervention to keep money cheap than by anything else. The great bull markets in history started when prices were irrationally cheap. It is difficult to say that this was true in March 2009. Surveys of investors did show great fear at the time—of populist anger, choking off of free trade, and the untried President Obama. But throughout history, stocks were much cheaper, and the economy in greater trouble, before great rallies began. A reliable long-term measure is the cyclically adjusted price/earnings ratio, first conceived by Benjamin Graham and more recently championed by Robert Shiller of Yale University. This metric compared share prices to average earnings over the previous 10 years, and correctly identified 1929 and 2000 as the two points when the U.S. stock market was the most crazily overvalued in history. It also spotted market lows. The cyclically adjusted Price Earnings Ratio (p/e) reached 5.5 before markets recovered in 1932, and almost 7 before the rally of 1982 (see Figure 9.5).[4]

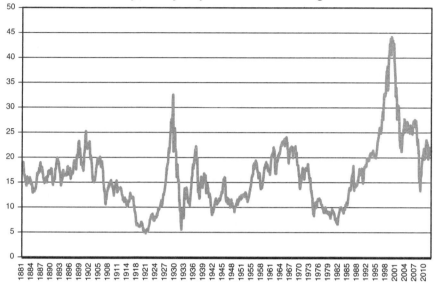

FIGURE 9.5   *The cyclically adjusted Price Earnings Ratio (p/e)
reached 5.5 before markets recovered in 1932 and almost dropped
to 7 before the rally of 1982. Is it significant that it never fell below
13 in the months after Lehman Brothers?*

In 2009, the cyclically adjusted p/e never fell below 13,
suggesting stocks needed to be halved once more before
they presented a truly compelling buying opportunity.
By the end of that year, it had settled back above 20,
where it remained until the summer of 2012—well
above the historic average and in line with its level on
the eve of Lehman. All this implies that the desperate
measures to save the banking system lifted the stock
market before speculative excess had been squeezed out.

And that is easy to believe. It is, after all, exactly what happened in 2003, when cheap money from the Fed arrested the decline in stocks and ignited the credit bubble, before the system had squeezed out the effects of the Dot-Com bubble. As the chart shows, the 2003 rebound came, otherwise incomprehensibly, when stocks were still historically expensive.

Investors show no signs of enthusiasm, despite all the money that has been made in the U.S. stock market. Indeed, one commentator described the great post-2009 rebound as "the most hated rally in Wall Street history."[5] Traders watched constantly for the next big Lehman-like event. Their vocabulary changed. After the Greek crisis broke out in full force in spring 2010, each day became known as either *risk-on* or *risk-off*. On risk-on days, investors bought European bonds, along with stocks, commodities, and emerging market currencies; when risk was "off," they sold these things and bought the dollar. Correlations grew ever tighter—even between assets that historically had had little link to each other—suggesting that all of them were priced inefficiently. Late in 2011, the long-term correlation between the dollar and commodities reached its highest in a decade, according to Brown Brothers Harriman. Meanwhile, correlation between the U.S. stocks in the S&P 500 reached an all-time record of 90 percent according to Goldman Sachs, suggesting equities moved "nearly completely in unison."[6] As traders cynically put it, deciding to buy anything involved answering one question: "What are the chances we go to hell?"

It grew ever harder to beat the market using an "active" strategy—picking individual stocks, rather than just tracking a major index. So active investors tended to match the index ever more closely, and many retail investors opted simply to match the index, rather than even attempt to find bargains. Investment in exchange-traded funds—bundles of shares that replicate an index and can be traded minute-by-minute throughout the day—hit new records, providing a further force for correlation. Total assets managed by such funds, the ultimate passive investments, were 75 percent greater in late 2011 than they had been at the market's peak in late 2007.[7]

Fund managers who wanted to keep their jobs had no choice. They needed to be part of the action, to avoid embarrassment. More than ever, they were benchmarked against the index, and because of the money in ETFs, an ever larger chunk of the market automatically chased prices higher. Even as the Eurozone crisis dragged on, the memory of the 2009 relief rally inhibited temptations to sell. Nobody wanted to miss out on any repeat of such a rally, and—after the disasters of 2008—nobody trusted themselves to bet on what politicians would do next. Low bond yields pushed them into stocks; financial repression forced them into bonds. The result: Investors kept markets in a state of suspended animation, rallying on reductions in risk and falling when risks seemed to increase.

Meanwhile, moral hazard—or the temptation to take excessive risks when people know they have insurance or protection—was greater than ever before. After the disastrous U.S. attempt to beat moral hazard by letting Lehman Brothers go bankrupt, the market assumed that in any game of chicken the government would swerve—and finance a rescue. And it looked like they were right. The Fed even promised not to raise rates until 2013. This was a key difference from the bear market lows of 1932 and 1982. On those occasions, financial pain had seen many firms fail and squeezed moral hazard out of the system. Investors were humbled. But in 2009, politicians consciously reignited risk-taking. The alternative to revisit the worst depths of 1932 seemed too dangerous and too painful.

The moral hazard alternative has—arguably—worked so far. Outside the Eurozone, most economies recovered more quickly than seemed possible in 2008. In the United States, consumers and banks have begun to sort out their outstanding piles of debt. But governments must at some point begin to repay the debts they took on to dig out of the crisis. That could mean austerity policies to reduce their spending—and the Eurozone has shown what an ugly effect that has on the economy. Or it means more financial repression, implying a long-running drag both on the markets for assets and on the world's economies. Whatever happens, governments will have to extract that money from somewhere. All of this is in line with history. After a financial implosion like 2008, a long period of volatile but fundamentally sideways movement by stock markets is the best anyone should expect.

And in any case, the moral hazard option is a risky game. The danger remains that another, more severe financial dislocation will be needed to purge the markets of these distortions. If it does not come soon from Europe, it could come later from China or the United States.

Summary

The recovery in the U.S. stock market since 2009—and its ability to withstand the crisis in Europe—has been driven by the low interest rates of the Federal Reserve, by moral hazard, and by the herding mentality of the modern investment industry.

- Tight correlations suggest markets are still priced inefficiently.

- Stocks were never as cheap at the bottom of the market as they were after previous great crashes.

- Neither the economy nor asset prices have sustained recoveries without new injections of central bank liquidity.

- High bond prices show that governments are resorting to financial repression.

- Markets remain "risk-on/risk-off": securities are priced according to the risks created by the crisis, not their fundamentals.

Endnotes

1. See "Financial repression: Then and now" by Carmen M Reinhart, Jacob Funk Kirkegaard. VOX, March 26, 2012: http://www.voxeu.org/article/financial-repression-then-and-now.

2. See "The Long Good Buy: The Case for Equities" by Peter Oppenheimer. Goldman Sachs International, https://360.gs.com.

3. See "Markets: Out of Stock" by John Authers and Kate Burgess. *Financial Times*, May 23, 2012: http://www.ft.com/intl/cms/s/0/d754f94c-a4ba-11e1-9908-00144feabdc0.html.

4. All of these figures are available at Professor Shiller's website: http://www.irrationalexuberance .com/index.htm.

5. See "The Most Hated Rally in Wall Street History" by Barry Ritholtz: http://www.ritholtz.com/blog/ 2009/10/the-most-hated-rally-in-wall-street-history/.

6. See "Correlation Dislocation; Drivers & Implications" by Christian Mueller-Glissmann. Goldman Sachs International, https://360.gs.com.

7. See ETGI global ETF and ETP industry insights, available at www.etfgi.com.

Chapter 10

2012 and After

The interests of beneficiaries are largely interests in long-term absolute performance. The concern of asset managers—and the basis on which they are monitored by many asset holders and by advisers to asset holders and retail investors—is short-term relative perform-ance. This misalignment of incentives creates many problems.

—John Kay, in *The Kay Review of Equity Markets and Long-Term Decision Making*[1]

Europe's crisis removes any possible belief that the disaster of 2007–09 has cured the world's finan-cial problems. They remain acute and must still be addressed even if, as is quite possible, the world nav-igates the next few years without a second major col-lapse in the prices of stocks, real estate, or other assets. For that to happen, even if the Eurozone avoids a disor-derly collapse, twin planks of the recovery—China's insatiable demand and the ability of big U.S. banks to "muddle through"—must stay in place. Both of those look shaky.

The most pressing question remains: Can Europe avoid its own "Lehman moment"? The answer is that it can, but not through austerity or through any financial engineering. Judged as a whole, the Eurozone has lower deficits than the United States or the United Kingdom. If Germany (and the region's other stronger economies) is prepared to stand behind all Eurozone debt, the pressure will disappear. The obstacles to this are purely political, but they are high, as they involve real concerns over national sovereignty.

If Germany were to underwrite the rest of Europe without making any conditions, it would create moral hazard. Those who had borrowed irresponsibly would escape any consequences. It is reasonable, then, to demand tougher financial oversight. But that means weaker European nations must accept that other countries, who already control their currency and their interest rates through the EU, must also take greater control over their public spending and taxes.

Both the center and the periphery need to compromise. This is always difficult on matters of such high principle. But so many technical issues are involved that compromises should be possible—if the politicians can give themselves enough time. Presumably there will ultimately be "euro-bonds," underwritten jointly by all the nations of the Eurozone. How would they work and who would issue them? Would there be a European finance ministry or a European finance minister? If so, how would they be elected? And for the banks central to the problem, does this mean pan-European banking regulation as well? No wonder politicians are desperate to buy time.

If the Eurozone cannot be reformed to make it tighter and more of a unit, an alternative is to make it smaller. Central bankers and finance ministers have provided numerous hints that they would be happy to see Greece leave the Eurozone. Portugal and Ireland might also be allowed to leave. Allowing this to happen would create difficult technical issues, but these need not be insuperable. The deepest problem is that this would create a precedent and encourage traders to bet on other countries to leave. Could the Eurozone survive in any meaningful way without Spain or Italy? They are the third and fourth largest economies in the euro. And if they were to leave, it is not at all clear that the world financial system could survive such an event without a crisis as least as severe as the one that followed the Lehman bankruptcy. Plenty of international banks hold their bonds.

If the Eurozone cannot be reformed or made smaller, one last feasible option would be to make the euro far weaker. Originally set so that one euro would equal one dollar, the euro remained resilient throughout the crisis and was worth \$1.25 even as the Greeks held their election in June 2012. There is room for it to weaken. Foreign exchange markets can do this themselves by pushing down the value of the euro, and the European Central Bank could do it by throwing aside its mandate and deliberately printing money to weaken the currency.[2] Inflation would make the problem countries' debts cheaper and easier to service. The weaker currency would also help protect Europe's industries from imports while boosting exports. Just as the United States and China have enjoyed a healthier post-Lehman recovery than the rest of the world by keeping their currencies artificially weak, Europeans could pull themselves out of the difficulties those countries created for them with their own devaluation.

A devaluation is never a healthy way to promote growth. It would doubtless cause other dominoes to fall, notably by making life harder for a U.S. exporting industry that had been returning to health. But if the alternative is to allow the Eurozone to suffer a disorderly collapse, it might well be preferable for everyone, including the Americans and the Chinese.

The ECB itself is the reason why this option has not already been attempted. First, it is dedicated by its mandate, and by its history, to fighting inflation. Printing new money to buy back debt runs counter to that. Second, as the ECB is backed by the Eurozone's taxpayers, any big debt purchase by the ECB would mutualize

Europe's debts "by stealth." The core countries' taxpayers might suffer the effects through higher inflation. But again, it is always possible to find compromises when issues are so technical—Outright Monetary Transactions, announced by the ECB in September 2012 to keep government bond yields down, show the possibilities. Given sufficient will and ingenuity, the ECB, like any central bank, should be able to help force its currency's exchange rate lower.

The best reason to hope for some technical compromise, perversely, is that the alternative is close to unthinkable. A disorderly collapse of the Eurozone would trigger a banking collapse and a depression to rival the 1930s. Politicians know this, and such a terrifying scenario can only concentrate minds.

Without some definitive resolution, the pattern of volatile markets dragging sideways with alternating waves of optimism and pessimism will continue. The risk of disaster remains small, but it is well above zero. And even if all-out disaster is avoided, both a deflationary recession driven by austerity (which was already unfolding in the summer of 2012), or resurgent inflation as central bankers give up and print money, appeared to be real possibilities. Hedging against both at once is impossible.[3] Hence, investors have stayed frozen in their tracks.[4]

Either outcome would have an impact on the rest of the world. The Eurozone is far too big an economy to be ignored. And yet, after all the dreadful European events described in this book, U.S. stocks remain more than double their lows following the Lehman crash. What does this imply? A severe recession for Europe is unavoidable, so the bet appears to be not only that catastrophic break-up of the euro can be avoided, but that the U.S. economy can continue to prosper even with Europe in deep recession. That looks mighty hopeful.

At a deeper level, the rest of the world also has its challenges. There is an overhang of debt that must be repaid, and all the ways to do this—which boil down to default, inflation, or accepting slow economic growth for many years—involve pain. And the flaws in the financial system would be difficult to fix at the best of times. They tend to involve putting limits on banks and their freedom to lend, which can easily mean disruptions to the supply of credit, and pain for millions. Politicians grow yet more reluctant to attempt this at a time when the economy is weak.

Averting disaster in the near-term will depend on politicians. Averting a repetition of these crises longer into the future will require a cultural shift. That will be difficult. Investment decisions are rooted in human behavior. The incentives to herd created by the investing industry in the last half-century intensified tendencies already embedded deep in human nature. As humans, we tend to move together, grow overconfident, and hope that others will rescue us from the consequences of our actions. Fixing such problems will take many years. The key is to change investors' incentives so that they treat others' money as if it were their own. In more technical terms, moral hazard must be removed.

Previous financial crises dealt with moral hazard by inflicting grievous losses on key investors. This one is different—by showing that the United States and then European governments would spend trillions of dollars to sustain big financial groups and even countries that had run out of money, the belief that risk-takers will be rescued is stronger than it was before. Air must be taken out of markets that are currently betting that the government dare not let them fail. It is hard to do this in the midst of a crisis. But at some point, either by raising rates or by allowing a big bank to go down, governments must make clear they will not be there to bail out risk-takers. One way to do this, much discussed, would be to force the biggest "too big to fail" banks to split.

A further problem remains: the banking industry has lost its old roles and, like unemployed teenage boys, banks have shown a terrible knack for getting into trouble when they are left to their own devices. It is questionable whether the economy even needs banks in their current, familiar form. Hedge funds drove many trends to destruction by 2007, but the much-feared disorderly collapse of a big hedge fund did not occur. Instead, it was the inherent instability of banks that brought the roof down in the United States and brought Europe to crisis. The larger hedge funds should continue their evolution to take on more and more of the functions of banks—structured as limited partnerships, where principals' wealth depends on their long-term success, they already look more like old-fashioned investment banks. That way, they should, at least, treat the money they put at risk as if it is their own. And as they are smaller than universal banks like JPMorgan, there is much more chance that managers will spot big risks before their traders have taken them too far.

As for investment managers, the key may be in the way they are paid and ranked. Rank them against their peers and an index, and pay them by how much money they manage—as at present—and they mindlessly hug ever closer to key benchmarks like the S&P 500. So we must change the way we pay fund managers. For hedge funds, which are not closely regulated, it is up to the market to refuse to pay fees on the skewed basis that adheres at present. At present, their pay encourages them to gear up to "go for broke" each year—which can lead them into the big bets against currencies and sovereign bonds that in themselves create a crisis. Paying fixed fees, with performance fees only payable after a period of much longer than one year, makes more sense.

In mutual funds, it is too easy for mediocrities to make money in an upward market by sticking to the stocks in the index. This might be discouraged by forcing funds to publish their "active share" (the amount their portfolio deviates from the stocks in the index).[5] Paying a fixed fee would no longer reward accumulating assets for its own sake, so funds would be less likely to grow too big. And rewards above a fixed fee should be for truly exceptional performance—although determining how to measure that is difficult.

The greatest power rests with regulators and the incentives they give to those who make big asset allocation decisions—the managers of big financial institutions and pension fund consultants. At present, regulators seem concerned primarily to push institutions to buy government debt—*financial repression*. Subtler regulations, giving institutions greater freedom to try to identify investment management skill and to reward it, would help very much.

Academics must also shoulder some responsibility. Their old theory of diversification prompted overconfidence. Core assumptions, such as stable correlations over time, random returns, and emphasis on allocation by asset classes, have failed and must go. Accidents such as JPMorgan's huge trading loss in May 2012 show that old models continue to guide behavior. We need a new theory.

That work has already started, inspired by sources from anthropology through thermodynamics to Darwinian biology.[6] But any new model must not aspire to the same precision as the old; finance and economics are contingent on human decision making and cannot be measured as precisely as physics. This should avert a return to the overconfidence such models created in the past. Instead, financiers and traders must use their own judgment.[7]

All these ideas involve putting limits on the wealth that markets can create, along with the profits that banks can make. It is understandable that the financial services industry objects. But this would be just like the trade-off the world made after the Depression, and many would now be happy to make it.

These are deep cultural changes. It is hard to think about them amid the hubbub created by the Eurozone crisis. But these issues, too, must be addressed, and the sooner the better. At the time of writing, the current crisis has dragged on for some five years; it is not over, and it has crossed the Atlantic. Its root cause was a series of asset bubbles across the world caused by flaws in the way the modern banking and investment industries had come to operate. Such speculative excesses are a fact of human nature, but for most of history they only happened once every one or two generations. When this crisis is resolved—and one day it will be—it would be good if the world could go two generations without another new bubble.[8]

Endnotes

1. Commissioned by the U.K. government and available online at: http://www.bis.gov.uk/assets/biscore/business-law/docs/k/12-917-kay-review-of-equity-markets-final-report.pdf.

2. For an interesting take on this, see "Long View: Time for a Change?" ft.com interview with Ian Harnett of Absolute Strategy Research: http://video.ft.com/v/1343360840001/Long-View-Time-for-a-change-.

3. See "Long View: What do bears invest in?," ft.com interview with Dylan Grice of Societe Generale. http://video.ft.com/v/1343313401001/Long-View-What-do-bears-invest-in-.

4. Bank of America Merrill Lynch surveys of fund managers, for example, have persistently shown investors lack conviction.

5. See "How Active is Your Fund Manager? A New Measure that Predicts Performance," by K.J. Martijn Cremers and Antti Petajisto. March 31, 2009: http://papers.ssrn.com/sol3/papers.cfm?abstract_id =891719.

6. See "Wanted: new model for markets" by John Authers. *Financial Times*, September 29, 2009.

7. See, for example, *A Call for Judgement, Sensible Finance for a Dynamic Economy* by Amar Bhide. Oxford University Press, 2010.

8. *The Fearful Rise* has a more detailed discussion of the issues around incentives for investment managers raised in this chapter.

INDEX

Index **163**

devaluation, 15, 151-153
Dimon, Jamie, 87, 90
Dodd-Frank Act, 86
Dow Jones Industrial Average,
        biggest fall of, 38
Draghi, Mario, 120

E

ECB (European Central Bank),
        119-120, 152
EFSF (European Financial Stability
        Facility), 103, 106
emerging markets, decoupling
        of, 43-51
ETFs (exchange-traded funds), 143
euro, 7
    genesis of, 11-24
    joining, 14
    possible devaluation of, 151-153
euro-bonds, 118, 123, 150
European banks
    bailouts, 36
    confidence, 35
European Central Bank (ECB), 14,
        119-120, 152
    lack of measures to bolster
        confidence in banks, 68-77
European Financial Stability
        Facility (EFSF), 103, 106
European Monetary System (EMS),
        14-17
European stock market, 58
Eurozone sovereign debt crisis, 1-2
    attempts by EU to quell crisis,
        101-107
    future, 150-159
    Greece, 3, 95-103, 107-108
    International Monetary Fund's
        World Economic Outlook,
        97-98
    Ireland, 98, 104
    Italy, 100
    member default, 4-5
    resulting political problems
        France, 122
        Germany, 123

Greece, 113-117, 125
Ireland, 116
Italy, 117
Portugal, 116
Spain, 116, 121-123
Portugal, 99, 104
Spain, 99-100
exchange rates, 14
    Germany, 21
    Spain, 21
exchange-traded funds (ETFs), 143

F

"fair value" accounting, 73-74
fall of banks, 34-40
fear, 29
The Fearful Rise of Markets, 1
Federal Reserve
    purchase of commercial
        paper, 70
    swap lines, 48
financial repression, 138-139, 157
fixed-asset investment (China), 57
forex, 45
France
    impact of Eurozone debt crisis
        on, 107
    political problems caused by
        financial crisis, 122
Fuld, Dick, 27
fund managers, 156
funds
    exchange-traded funds
        (ETFs), 143
    fund managers, 156
    hedge funds, 155
    mutual funds, 157
future of Eurozone, 150-159

G

Germany
    Deutsche Mark, 17
    exchange rates, 21
    fall of banks, 39
    interest rates, 15